THIS IS SMART MONEY THINKING

PUZZLES & QUOTES

THIS IS SMART

HUBARATO SAIKARO

Copyright © 2023 LinguaLibros

All rights reserved.

Cover *by Yossi Matbil* with the assistance of BlueWillow

❀ Created with Vellum

In honor of Daikokuten, the god of wealth

CONTENTS

Introduction   vii

WILLIAM (BILL) ACKMAN   1
BERNARD BARUCH   35
KYLE BASS   67
CARL ICAHN   101
JAMES (JIM) CHANOS   135
RAYMOND (RAY) DALIO   171
NICHOLAS DARVAS   207
JESSE LIVERMORE   241
CHARLES (CHARLIE) MUNGER   277
JAMES (JIM) ROGERS   311
GEORGE SOROS   347
EDUARD (ED) THORP   379

About the Author   415
Books by Hubarato Saikaro   417
Solutions   419

INTRODUCTION

"This Is Smart Money Thinking" is not your typical book of humorous money quotes, sayings, and anecdotes. While it certainly offers that delightful aspect, it goes beyond mere entertainment. This book presents a unique approach to personal growth and financial wisdom. By engaging with just one thought-provoking snippet of wisdom each day and reflecting on its profound meaning, you can transform yourself into a wiser trader and investor over the course of a year.

Let the presence of Daikokuten, the god of wealth, accompany you on this enriching journey through the pages of this beautiful collection of quotes. These words of wisdom will not only brighten your days but also serve as valuable guidance in your pursuit of both enjoyment and profit in the financial world.

For each day, the book gives you an inspiring quote and a Sudoku puzzle, carefully selected to further stimulate and train your mind. This combination of mental exercises and financial insights creates a holistic and engaging reading experience.

To enhance your experience, the publisher offers a downloadable PDF containing the puzzles and their solutions, ensuring that

INTRODUCTION

you have everything you need to fully immerse yourself in the book.

Get ready to embark on a path towards financial success, guided by the wisdom within these pages. Let "This Is Smart Money Thinking" be your companion on this rewarding journey. Enjoy and embrace the possibilities that lie ahead!

To your financial success!

Hubarato Saikaro

THE SUDOKU PUZZLE

The goal of a Sudoku puzzle is to fill out each row, column and square with the numbers 1-9, without repeating any numbers within the row, column or square.

4	7		3	6		8	5		1	4	7	9	3	6	2	8	5
	9	3		8		7	6		5	9	3	1	8	2	7	6	4
8		2	7		5	3	9	1	8	6	2	7	4	5	3	9	1
	1		9	7		4			3	1	8	6	9	7	5	4	2
4		3	5				6	➡	4	2	9	3	5	1	8	7	6
7		6		8		3			7	5	6	4	2	8	1	3	9
2	7		8	6	9	4		3	2	7	1	8	6	9	4	5	3
			5			2			9	8	4	5	1	3	6	2	7
6	3		2			9	1	8	6	3	5	2	7	4	9	1	8

WILLIAM (BILL) ACKMAN

Born William Albert Ackman on May 11, 1966, he grew up in a wealthy Jewish family in New York. His father was chair of a prominent real estate financing firm, the Ackman-Ziff Real Estate Group.

In 1988, he earned a *magna cum laude* bachelor of arts degree in history from Harvard University. He got his MBA in 1992.

Partnering with his classmate David Berkowitz he launched his first hedge fund, Gotham Partners. He grew up on his family extensive network to provide the financing for the company. Early investors included Seth Klarman, Michael Steinhardt, and Whitney Tilson.

Gotham had $500 million in assets by 1998 but was closed down in 2002 after a problematic and litigious investment in a golf course that ultimately ended with investors asking for the return of their capital.

In 2004, he started hedge fund Pershing Square Capital Management with $54 million assets under management. Typically, the fund invests in only a handful of substantial positions.

Some of Ackman investments brought him a great deal of notoriety. His short position on bond insurer MBIA took several years to play out but brought in billions for Pershing in 2008. The saga chronicled in the book "Confidence Game" by Christine Richard.

He took a $1 billion short position against Herbalife, the nutritional supplements company, which he called a pyramid scheme that would eventually go to zero. Ackman had a notorious brawl on CNBC with Carl Icahn about Herbalife in 2013. The two traded insults, such as:

Ackman— "Carl Icahn, unfortunately, does not have a good reputation for being a handshake guy"

Icahn— "I wouldn't invest with you if you were the last man on Earth!" The battle about Herbalife is the subject of a documentary called "Betting on Zero."

Ackman made a disastrous investment in Valeant, a pharmaceutical company. In 2014 they launched a joint hostile bid for Allergan Pharmaceuticals that was unsuccessful. Ackman ended up acquiring a position in Valeant. That was in 2015, just before the company came under scrutiny for its use of a shady mail-order pharmacy. Since then the stock lost more than 90% of its value and triggered a mounting number of shareholder's suits, and further investigations into Valeant's practices. Ackman reportedly exited the position in 2017 selling his 27 million shares, whose average purchasing price was $196, at only $11 each.

1

The only difference between a tax man and a taxidermist is that the taxidermist leaves the skin.

— MARK TWAIN

2			9	7	8	4	6	3
4				6			2	
		6			2		4	
6	2	5		7	9	1	8	3
9	4					5	6	2
		3		5				4
5		4		3	7	2	1	
				2	1	4		
1	6		9	4	5			

1

2

The best time to buy anything is last year.

— UNKNOWN

6	9		1		5	7		4
3				2		8	6	9
		7	8		9	1	3	
			5		6			
1			4	7	3			2
7		4	9		2			6
4		3	2	9	7			
			2	6				1
			6		4		9	

3

The next trade is the most important trade of your life.

— MARTY SCHWARTZ

		5			8	9		1
		7	1			6		
1		4	5	3	6		8	7
			4	1		3	6	5
	1			5		7		
5			8	7	2		9	
		3	2	8	7		1	
		2	9	4	1	5		
	4		3	6	5			

4

Don't focus on making money; focus on protecting what you have.

— PAUL TUDOR JONES

8	3	1	4	6		2	5	
	6		7	2		3	1	8
	2		8		1		9	
9	7				3	4		1
5								
1	4		9	7	2	8	3	
				5	8		4	
		8				9		
3	1							

5

An investment in knowledge pays the best interest.

— BENJAMIN FRANKLIN

	8	3	5		2	6		4	1
		6		4	1		5		
				3					
		2			4		3		8
		7						2	
			3	6				7	4
	6			1	7	4	8		5
	4	1	7	5	8	3	6		
									7

5

6

Who has a lot of money, can speculate. Who has little money, must not speculate. Who has no money, must speculate.

— ANDRÉ KOSTOLANY

2		3	9				7	4
8	9	5	4				6	
4	1	7					5	
7				2	6	8		5
3	2	6			5			7
5	8		7	4	1	3	2	
1				6		2	5	
		2	5				4	1
	5				4	6		

7

Cash is a fact; profit is an opinion.

— ALFRED RAPPAPORT

	2			7				
		7		6	5		1	2
5		6	3		2	7		9
		4	2	3	1		7	8
	1	2			7	5		6
7		9		4	6	2		
	6	5	1				9	
	3			7		6		
9	7							3

8

Money is not the prime asset in life. Time is.

— GORDON GEKKO (MICHAEL DOUGLAS), WALL STREET: MONEY NEVER SLEEPS

8		6	2	3		7		5
4				9		7		6
		5			8			
	7	1				5	4	9
	8			9	5		7	
	4		7	1		3	8	
	6	8						
	3	4	5		1	2	6	
1			6	8	2	9		

8

9

Government-Sponsored bumper sticker: drive carefully, we need every taxpayer we can get.

— UNKNOWN

						8		4
						1	3	
		9			3			6
	4	8			1	6	5	3
							8	7
		5	7	4		1		
					4	9		8
			8	9	2	3	6	1
8	9	2	1					

9

10

The poor looks for food and the rich man for appetite.

— INDIAN PROVERB

4		3		7	1			
1	5					6		
		2	6				7	1
7	4	5	1	9	2			3
2	1	9	8	6				
3	8	6		5			9	
	7	1	2			3		
6	2	8			4	5		
5						9	2	

10

11

When somebody says it's not about the money, it's about the money.

— H. L. MENCKEN

			1	3		4		5
		5			9		1	3
	9	2		1	7	3		
7	8			6	3		9	
		4	9					1
	7	8	3	4		5		
				5		2		
6	5		7	8		1		

12

Bulls make money. Bears make money. Pigs get slaughtered.

— WALL STREET SAYING

1	2	8			3	9		5
		6		5	9			
5					8	6		
6	7	3	9		5			
4	5	9		1		3		7
			3	6			9	4
	4			8	1	7	3	
2		1	7		6		5	
	6					1		

13

You only need a few good stocks in your lifetime. I mean how many times do you need a stock to go up ten-fold to make a lot of money? Not a lot.

— PETER LYNCH

				7	9			
3	7		5		1	6	4	2
	1	5		6				8
	9	7				6	3	4
2			4	8	3	5		7
				7		2	6	1
		6		7				
	5	3				4	8	
1		9				7		

13

14

I don't want to be a millionaire; just live like one.

— WALTER HAGEN

						9		8
7		2		9	4	1		
		9	1	6	3			5
9	4				1	5		
6	3			2	7		9	
	7	5			9			6
		7		4				1
8		4						2
1	6		7	5		4	8	

14

15

Assets require more scrutiny than the liabilities.

— CHARLIE MUNGER

			5		6			1
			6	3			5	4
	3		8					7
	2				7	6		
					1		4	2
			1					9
			9	1				
				5	2		7	6
		2	4	6		3	1	

15

16

It's money. I remember it from when I was single.

— BILLY CRYSTAL

4		9		1		5	3	
	1	8	3	6		9	4	
	6	5		2	9			
9	4			7		1		
	7		5			6	9	4
		1	9			2	8	7
2			1	5	7			9
1				9		4	2	
6		3						

16

17

Experience taught me to listen to one's gut, no matter how good something sounds on paper; that one's generally better off sticking with what one knows, and that sometimes the best investments are the ones you don't make.

— DONALD TRUMP

1		9		4	8	6		
		8					1	7
3	2		1					
		4			6			
			9				4	8
9	1	7	8		4			
	9	1	4	8	5			6
		5		3		7		
	6	3			1	5		

18

I hate weekends because there is no stock market.

— RENE RIVKIN

			1	7		4	8	
9		6	8	2				6
			9	3		5	1	7
2		8	6				5	1
	9	3				2		
5		7				6		
			5	1		3		
			3	6	9	1	7	
3			7		1	8		

18

19

One common adage...that is completely wrongheaded is: You can't go broke taking profits. That's precisely how many traders do go broke. While amateurs go broke by taking large losses, professionals go broke by taking small profits.

— WILLIAM ECKHARDT

9		2	8		6	1		
			4	1	7			5
			5			3		
	7	8						6
		4		5	3		1	7
	6	5			1			9
5	3		1	6	8		4	
8		6				9	5	3
				9	5		8	1

20

Once upon a time in a remote land, a stranger turned up and announced that he would buy monkeys for $10 each. The natives rushed out to the forest and started catching them.

The man bought thousands of monkeys at $10, and as supply started to diminish, the villagers stopped their effort. He then let it know that he was now a buyer at $20. This promise motivated the villagers, who resumed catching monkeys.

After a few days, the supply diminished even further, and the villagers started losing interest. The man increased his offer to

$25 each, and the number of monkeys became so little that it was difficult enough to find a monkey, let alone to catch one!

The man raised his price to $50! He then let it know that since he had to go to the city on business, his assistant would purchase on his behalf.

After he left, the assistant tempted the villagers: "Look, I will sell you all the monkeys the man left in this cage at $35. When he comes back from the city, you can sell them to him for $50 each." The villagers eagerly dug up all their savings and bought all the monkeys in the cage.

They never saw the man nor his assistant again. That's how the stock market works.

— UNKNOWN

	4	9	1			2	5	7
		6	1		7	8		9
2	5		9			1		6
9		4	6	1				
	3	6	7		5	9		4
7	2	5			8	6	1	
5			8	4	9		6	
	9			6		5		
			5					8

21

Adversity makes a man wise, not rich.

— ROMANIAN PROVERB

	5	8			2			
	6			4				5
4	7	1	5	8		6	9	
8	3	5		6	9	7		
	2		7			5		
	4	7	3			2		
	9	2		7	1	3	5	8
7	1			3	5	9	2	
5			9	2				1

22

The three most harmful addictions are heroin, carbohydrates, and a monthly salary.

— NASSIM TALEB

9				4		6		
6	4				1	5	9	2
8	1		9	2	3			
5	8			9	2			
3		2		4	7			
7	6	4	5				3	
	7		1	5		9	2	
	5			3	9	4		6
2			7	6		1		

21

23

My basic advice is: don't lose money!

— JIM ROGERS

	4	7	1		3	5	6	
3	1		6		5			2
	6	9	7			1		3
	3					4		
	5						1	8
	2			1	8			
6	9		2	4		8		1
		2	8	3		6	9	5
				5	6	7		

22

24

Anticipation is key to investing and to business generally. You can't wait for an opportunity to become obvious.

— EDDIE LAMPERT

		4	6	7	5	1	3	9	8
7			1	9		3	6		
9			3		4	6	1		5
		2		6		5			9
6							4	3	2
			8						7
4			7		1		2	8	3
5							7	4	
		3	2		6				1

23

25

I never attempt to make money on the stock market. I buy on the assumption that they could close the market the next day and not reopen it for five years.

— WARREN BUFFETT

			8	7	1	4		6
9								
8		1	6		3		9	
		3			9	1		7
	6							
	9			8	7	6		3
1	8	7	3					9
					8	3	6	
7	1		4	3	6			
			2	9	5	8		

26

If you try to watch the stock market every day you go blind.

— UNKNOWN

3		1	7	8				4
		7		6		5		
					1	2		
1	3	5	2	7		4	6	9
	8	2	9					1
4	6	9	1			8	2	
	7			9				
9						7	8	2
5	1		8					

25

27

One of the funny things about the stock market is that every time one person buys, another sells, and both think they are astute.

— WILLIAM FEATHER

	4		5		3	2	7	
1	3			2	7	4	9	
	7	6		4		3	5	
	8	4			1			
	1			6			4	9
			9		4		3	
	9					7	6	2
3		1		7		9	8	
7		2	4					

26

28

Capitalism without Bankruptcy is like Christianity without Hell - it does not work.

— KYLE BASS

	8	3	4		5	2		
4	7		2	9			8	3
2	9				3			5
				2	9	1		8
	2	9			8		4	
1		8	3			5	2	
	1	6		3	4	7		2
				5		9	1	
			2	9	6			4

27

29

A bargain is something you can't use at a price you can't resist.

— FRANKLIN JONES

	6	8			5	1	3	
9	5	2				6		
	1	3		4		5	2	9
		5				6		
			6	8				
	7	6	5	2		9	1	
5			9			7		
		9		6		4		
6	3			5		2	9	

28

30

The market does not beat them. They beat themselves, because though they have brains they cannot sit tight.

— JESSE LIVERMORE

	1			3				
		3			5		4	1
	5		8		4	9		
	2	9					1	6	4
	8							3
	4	1			9	3	2	5	7
		8		4	1		3	2
	6	4				9	3	8
	3			5	7		4	

29

31

If small money does not go out, big money will not come in.

— CHINESE PROVERB

			5			9		3
	5	6	3	9				
2				1				5
1				5	6	3	9	4
	7	5	4			8	1	
				8		5	6	
3		4	9		8			
8	9			7		4	3	6
	1	7					8	9

BERNARD BARUCH

Bernard Mannes Baruch was born in 1870 and graduated from the College of the City of New York in 1889.

A.A. Houseman and Company, a brokerage firm, hired him as a runner[1]. A quick study, smart and intelligent, the Jewish boy quickly became a broker and then a partner. He used his earnings to buy a seat in the New York Stock Exchange.

His cunning speculations in the sugar market made him a millionaire. By the age of 30, the fiercely independent Baruch had earned the nickname "The Lone Wolf of Wall Street," owned his brokerage firm, and was one of the most respected financiers of the city.

In 1916, Baruch accepted President Woodrow Wilson invitation to serve on the Advisory Commission to the Council of National Defense. He chaired the new War Industries Board from

1918 participated at the Paris Peace Conference. He was awarded the Army Distinguished Service Medal and received a citation for his services during the World War.

Notwithstanding that, widely circulated rumors accused him of profiting personally from the war. He was attacked by Henry Ford's "Dearborn Independent" newspaper. Ford believed he was involved in a Zionist plot to control the world.

During World War II he served as special adviser to the director of the Office of War Mobilization by appointment of President Roosevelt, of whom he remained a trusted adviser and confidant until his death.

At 75 Baruch accepted his last public nomination, as the American representative to the United Nations Atomic Energy Commission.

His habit of walking and sitting in public parks, where he discussed politics and government affairs with other people, earned him another nickname, the "Park bench statesman." On his ninetieth birthday, a commemorative park bench in Lafayette Park across from the White House was dedicated to him.

Baruch passed away in 1965 at the age of 94.

---

1. A runner was the employee who delivered trade orders to the floor trader for execution.

1

As a trader you often walk on the blade. Be careful and don't step off.

— MARC RICH

			3	7	2		5	4
	7			9	5	4	1		8
			9				6		
			4				2		
3	8			6			4	9	5
6	7			4					3
		6	7	5			3		
				8			7	2	6
				2		7			

31

2

I never said I was better than anyone, just more successful.

— @GSELEVATOR

6				5		4		7
4	5	3	7		8	9	1	
	7			6				
3				8		6		
2				1	6	4		3
1	6	9	4					
				8				5
9	1	6	3	4			2	8
5				2		7	6	9

32

3

Always borrow money from a pessimist, he doesn't expect to be paid back.

— UNKNOWN

			4	9			5	2
9			7		2	6	3	
5			6		8	4	9	1
4			8		3		6	9
7	3						4	5
6			2			8		
8		9		1		3	2	7
1		5			7			
2		3						

33

4

A stockbroker urged me to buy a stock that would triple its value every year. I told him:

"At my age, I don't even buy green bananas".

— CLAUDE D. PEPPER

5

Don't confuse brains with a bull market.

— HUMPHREY B. NEILL

5	1		6	8	2			4
8	2	6			3		5	
3	7	4		9	5	8		6
	5			6				7
	8	2			4			
	3	7	5	1	9			
	6		4			5	1	9
7		3	9		1	2	6	8
1					6		4	

35

6

A stockbroker is one who invests other people's money until it's all gone.

— WOODY ALLEN

1				8		7		2
6		3			2	1	4	5
	9	2		4	5	6	8	3
3			2	9				
	6		5			3	1	
	7	4	3					
8		1				4		
	3			2	7	8	5	1
				1		9		6

36

7

What good is the Moon? You can't buy it or sell it.

— IVAN BOESKY

5				4	9	8		3
			6			2	5	7
		8		7		9		4
								1
2	5	3		1		4	8	
9				6		3	2	
4			3	2			7	9
3		6			5		4	8
	9	5		8				

37

8

Since the dawn of capitalism, there has been one golden rule: "If you want to make money, you have to take risks."

— UNKNOWN

	7					3	6	2
4				3				5
		6	7	9	5	8		4
6					9			
9	5	3			1	2		6
1				2		6	5	9
3	9		1		7	6	4	
7		5	6	4		9	2	
8	6	4			3	1		

38

9

Stock market bubbles don't grow out of thin air. They have a solid basis in reality, but reality as distorted by a misconception.

— GEORGE SOROS

	7		5			8		
			6	9		1	3	5
	9	8		7		5	4	6	2
		7		5					6
		2	4		9	8			1
		9			7		2		
			2			9			
4		9					5	2	
8	1	7	3				6	9	

39

10

Deceive the rich and powerful if you will, but don't insult them.

— JAPANESE PROVERB

			5	4			9	
	5	4	3		9	6		
	3	7		6		4	2	5
	2	3						
6				5				
4		5	2			8		9
8					5			
	6			2		9		
3	4		7				5	6

40

11

I have enough money to last me the rest of my life unless I buy something.

— JACKIE MASON

		6	2	7				
7		2					3	6
	9		6	4		7	8	
	7		8		1			9
	1					2	7	3
6	4			2				8
		4	7	8		6	1	
8		7	1	9			2	
9		1				8	5	7

41

12

When friends and acquaintances are telling you that you are a genius, before you accept their opinion, take a moment to remember what you always thought of their opinions in the past.

— CARL ICAHN

5	1		3	4			2	6
			6			1		
			5	1	9	4		
2			9		7	3		
			8			6	4	2
8	3	1				5		9
4		3	7	9			5	
	9			8			3	
	8			2	3	9		

42

13

In investing, what is comfortable is rarely profitable.

— ROBERT ARNOTT

			2	8			6		9
					6	4	7		2
					2	7	3		8
	7	1	5	8			9	6	
3		8	4				2		
		4				2			5
8		5	6	4					
			2				5	8	3
1			3			8	4		

43

14

I always say that you could publish your trading rules in the newspaper, and no one would follow them. The key is consistency and discipline.

— RICHARD DENNIS

			2	5		3			1
				9				5	
	1			8		5		9	3
				9	4		1	6	2	5
	8				6	2			7	9
		6			7	9	3	1		
					5		2		3	7
		5	6		7					
	9					4		5	6	

44

15

Having money makes sense. And having sense makes money.

— UNKNOWN

		9		5				
8		5		1	4			3
7				6	9		8	2
5		2					6	
4	7				6	2		
9								
	4	7	6		3	8	2	5
						7	1	4
2		8	1		7			6

45

16

We are all wrong so often that it amazes me that we can have any conviction at all over the direction of things to come. But we must.

— JIM CRAMER

		7		4	6		8	2	5
	1	4	8	2		3	7	
5	8		7			1	4	6
4		1		8			3	
2		8				6		
9			1		6	5	8	2
	9			1				8
			2		8			
8		5	9					

46

17

If you can count your money, you don't have much.

— JOHN PAUL GETTY

4			6					3
6		1		2		9		
			4	9	7	8		6
			1	3			9	
	3		5			6	8	
5	4		7		8	3		
2		4		7		1	3	
			8	1	3			
					4		6	

47

18

The older I get, the more I see a straight path where I want to go. If you're going to hunt elephants, don't get off the trail for a rabbit.

— T. BOONE PICKENS

	1			8	9	5	2	
	8			4	2	7		3	1
		2	7		6	3	9	5	
			3	1			6	5
	1				6	4	9	
5				4		2		
	5	1	9				2
9	7	8		3		5		6
						7	8	

48

19

Most investors want to do today what they should have done yesterday.

— LAWRENCE SUMMERS

	2	3	4	8	1		5	9
		8					2	3
	5	9	2	3		8		
		5	6	2	3	4		1
3	6		1	4			7	5
8				9	7	6		
		7						
	3	6	8			5		7
			7		9		3	6

49

20

Money will buy you everything but good sense.

— JEWISH PROVERB

9		6	2				1	3
			3		1			6
	1	3	6		5			
		7			4	6	8	5
3	4	1		6	8			
6		5	7	2	9	3	4	
7			4	1			3	
1		4	8			7		
					6			4

50

21

If you have trouble imagining a 20% loss in the stock market, you shouldn't be in stocks.

— JACK BOGLE

			8			7		6
		5		7	2	3		
6	7				1		5	8
	6				7			
1		7	5	8	3	6		2
			2					1
				2		1	6	
	2					5	9	
7	1	6		5	9		8	

51

22

Bull markets are born on pessimism, grow on skepticism, mature on optimism, and die on euphoria.

— JOHN TEMPLETON

	4	6		8	1			
1	2	8	3		9	4	6	
		5			7	2		
			7		5	1	2	6
5	7				6	9		8
6	1	2	9	3	8	7	4	5
	8			7			1	
3	5				4	8	9	
						5		

52

23

If you count your pennies, your dollars will take care of themselves.

— UNKNOWN

3	1	9	6				7	5
		8		5	2			
	5		3	1				4
8								
		1		6				7
9	6		8	7	5	1	2	3
	8		5			6		9
5			1	9	6			8
		9	6	4		3	5	2

53

24

The whole world is simply nothing more than a flowchart for capital.

— PAUL TUDOR JONES

		6			5	1		
4	3			1	6		2	
1	7			2	9		3	
9			7	5	2	6	8	
		2		8				
8				4			1	
						2		
7	5		8	6	4		9	
6	8		4	9		7	5	

54

25

The investor of today does not profit from yesterday's growth.

— WARREN BUFFETT

		7				8		
5	3	4	6		8	1	2	
	6							4
						9	1	
4	8		1			7		3
9	1	2		3			8	6
						9		
3						7		5
6			7	5				

26

When you let money speak for you, it drowns out anything else you meant to say.

— MIGNON MCLAUGHLIN

					9	5		
9					5	2	8	
		3	1	2		4		7
	1	2	9			3	5	
4		7	5	6	3			
		3				7	4	9
	5			8	1	9	7	
2	1			7				5
	9			6				2

56

27

Experienced traders control risk, inexperienced traders chase gains.

— ALAN FARLEY

			4		9	5	1	7
		9	1		5			3
1		5	8			4		9
			6	8		9		
		8	9			7		1
9	4	2		1	7	3		8
			1		8	2	9	
	3		2			1	7	
2		4					3	6

57

28

A man calls his broker, who tells him that he's got a hot new stock pick. "Buy it, buy it," the man says.

The next day he calls the broker for an update – the stock is up 5%. "Buy it, but it," the man says.

The next day he calls the broker again, and the stock is up another 5%. "Buy some more, buy some more," the man says.

He calls the broker again the next day, who tells him the stock is up 10%. "Sell it, sell it," the man says.

The broker says: "To whom?"

— UNKNOWN

9			1			8	4	
							2	9
				2		5	1	
2	9	7		3		6		
	5	1					7	
8	4		9			3		1
	8			7				5
		9		5		4	6	
1	3	5	4		8	2		

175

29

This is worse than a divorce. I've lost half my net worth and I still have a wife.

— UNKNOWN

	4	1				9	6	
3	9			5	6	4		7
5					4			3
	7	9					4	1
	3	6						
	5	4		8	7	3	6	2
4	2					8		6
9	1	7	3	6		5		
6		3				7		

58

KYLE BASS

Kyle Bass was born in 1969 in Florida where his father managed the Fontainebleau Miami Beach, the most luxurious hotel in Miami Beach. They later moved to Dallas, Texas. Kyle attended the Texas Christian University in Fort Worth, earning in 1992 a B.B.A. in finance.

After graduating, he worked briefly at Prudential Securities before joining the now-defunct Bear Sterns, where he quickly rose to senior managing director. In 2001 Bass accepted Legg Mason's offer to open and run their institutional equity office in Texas. A few years later he started his hedge fund, Hayman Capital Management, L.P.

In early 2006, Bass saw clear signs of the developing residential real-estate bubble in the United States and predicted the imminent subprime mortgage crisis. He raised additional capital to invest in that opportunity, eventually managing four billion USD of positions in subprime residential mortgage-backed securities. He became a billionaire and gained a tremendous amount of notoriety in the financial services industry. Dallas' D Magazine profiled him in the article "Cashing in on Subprime."

After the subprime debt he started bets against sovereign debts stating that "Europe goes first, then Japan and finally the United States." In a doomsday speech he delivered in 2014, he predicted that "War is coming – just as it has throughout history."

He has a defensive plan for when the world crashes — buy guns and physical gold (he also likes platinum bars).

Besides roaming around his ranch in a fully weaponized US Army Jeep, he enjoys freediving and spearfishing.

1

Don't stay in bed unless you can make money in bed.

— GEORGE BURNS

		8		3	5		9	7
3	5	4			9			6
				8				
			5		3			9
4	3					6		
7	2	9	1	6				4
		4	3	2		1		
				8	1			
8				5		9		2

59

2

He who borrows gets sorrows.

— TURKISH PROVERB

	7	9	4	3	2	6		5
		3			8		1	7
5	6		7		1	2		
		3				7	9	
		6					2	
9	1	7			3	5	6	
			3	2	4	8		
3	2		6		5	1	7	
6				1	7	4	3	2

60

3

To make money in the markets, you have to think independently and be humble.

— RAY DALIO

				8	5	1	2	
				9			7	
	1	2		6			3	
		5		7		8	4	3
7	6	1		3				2
3			5	2		6		
5	2			1		6		
1		9		4		2		5
4	3	6					9	1

61

4

A man is usually more careful of his money than of his principles.

— OLIVER WENDELL HOLMES

6	4	3					5	7
2	1	9	5	7		3	6	4
		8	6	4				
9	5	7	8			1	3	2
			3	2		7	9	
	2					4		
	9			8	6	2	4	
				3	2			9
		2				6	7	8

62

5

MONEY, n. A blessing that is of no advantage to us excepting when we part with it. Evidence of culture and a passport to polite society. Supportable property.

— AMBROSE BIERCE

2						7	4	
		9	8	7	4	3	5	
				5			8		9
5	2	3			1	9	7	
8		6	9	7				2
7					2			1
			1	9	7	4		5
		1	4		5	2		8
	3	4			8			7

63

6

The key to trading success is emotional discipline. If intelligence were the key, there would be a lot more people making money trading... the single most important reason that people lose money in the markets is that they don't cut their losses short.

— VICTOR SPERANDEO

				9			7	4	8
	3				7		6	2	
		4	8			2			
5	7		3	9			1	4	
	6		4						2
8				5	7		6		
	7						9	1	
3				4	9	2		7	
4		1	7					6	

64

7

If hard work were such a wonderful thing, surely the rich would have kept it all to themselves.

— LANE KIRKLAND

	6	9		5	8	4	1	
5	8	2	4				6	
1	7		3		9		8	
	3			2		7		1
	5			4	1	9		
4		7						
			1			6		3
		1		9	3	8	2	5
			5			1	7	

65

8

Those who believe money can do everything are frequently prepared to do everything for money.

— UNKNOWN

		5	9	3	2	4		
				4				7
		8				9	3	2
			8		5		9	3
		5	7				4	1
7			2	4	1			5
		4	1	8	6			9
	8	6	5	7	9	3		4
	7	9	3			1	8	

66

9

The economy depends about as much on economists as the weather does on weather forecasters.

— JEAN-PAUL KAUFFMANN

2	3		6			8		5
6		9		8			4	
5			2		4	7		
4		8		6		5		1
		3		5		2		4
	5		4	2	8	6	3	
		6		4	5	9	2	
8			3	9				7
3			7	1	6			8

67

10

Wall Street people learn nothing and forget everything.

— BENJAMIN GRAHAM

```
4  2  9 │ 1
      5 │ 7     6        4
6       │       4 │ 1  5
────────┼─────────┼────────
3     2 │ 8  1   │ 6  7  5
      1 │ 6     5│       3
        │ 4  2  3│ 8
────────┼─────────┼────────
        │ 9  8   │
   9    │ 5  6  1│ 3     7
   5    │ 3      │       2
```

68

11

This market right now is moving on nothing more than emotions. Guess what? It almost always moves on emotions.

— DAVID BACH

4	8	5	1	2				3
1		9	3	6				
	6	7			5		9	
9	4	2		1			8	
7	1				8	4		9
	3	8	9	4	2	1		7
						9		
	2	5	6		1	7		8
			8	7		5		

69

12

When the rich make war, it's the poor that die.

— RUSSIAN PROVERB

5		2			7			3
							2	
			4	2	5	1		7
8	3	1		9				6
			7			3		
6	7	4	3				9	
4				7		2	3	9
	7			3	9		5	
9			6			8	7	1

70

13

Everyone has the brainpower to follow the stock market. If you made it through fifth-grade math, you can do it.

— PETER LYNCH

9		7	5		6	8		4
				3	4		2	7
8	3	4			7			
7			6	9	1	4		
		1				3		
						6	9	1
2				7	9	3	6	5
1	7	9		6	5	2		8
		6		4	8	1		

71

14

Buy on the rumor, sell on the news.

— WALL STREET SAYING

	3	6		8			1	
2			7	5		9	3	6
					9			4
				3			8	
			2	4		7		
8	2	4		7		6	9	
	8	2	5		7	3		
1	7		6		3			
		6		8				

72

15

What's considered enough money? Just a little bit more.

— WILL ROGERS

8		7	1		5		4	
9	5						8	3
4		6					9	
1	8	5		6		3	7	
		2	3		4			
	4	3	5	1	8			
			9	2	1	4		
2	1		4	3	6		5	
					7			

73

16

When an economist says the evidence is 'mixed', he or she means that theory says one thing and data says the opposite.

— RICHARD THALER

```
          |       |  3 2  |
    5     | 1 3   |       |
3 2 1 | 9 |       |     7 |
------+---+-------+-------+
      | 3 | 2 1   |  4    |
1 3   | 4 | 9 8   |  6    |
4     |   |   6   | 2     |
------+---+-------+-------+
  1   |   |   9   |     6 |
8   9 | 6 |       | 3     |
6 5 7 |   |       |   8.  |
```

74

17

It's easy to meet expenses – everywhere we go, there they are.

— UNKNOWN

4								
2	8			7		9		
	1	5			3		8	6
9	4	3					7	
	2	8		5				4
	7			9		6	2	8
		7	4	3		8		
	9				2	1	5	7
8	6	2		1				

75

18

Anybody who tells you money is the root of all evil doesn't fucking have any.

— JIM YOUNG (BOILER ROOM)

			7			3	4	
		7			2	1		6
3	4				1		5	7
		9	6	8		7	2	
			5			6	1	
			4		9		7	8	5
5			8			3		1
				6			7	8
6			9		8	5	4	2

76

19

Stocks are bought on expectations, not facts.

— GERALD M. LOEB

		9	6			2		1
6		4			2		7	
3			7		9	4		8
			4				2	
	6		2					
2	3			7	1	5	4	
1		3	5		7	6	8	2
	4	7	8		6		1	
8	2		1			7		

77

20

Never run after a bus or a stock. Be patient; the next one will come along for sure.

— ANDRÉ KOSTOLANY

		8	5		2	1	7	9
	5	3	9	1				4
7	9			8	6			5
	2		7	5	1	9		
1	7	5	6	9		4		2
	6			4				
9				6	4		5	
4	3							
5	1		8			6		3

78

21

I don't trade for excitement; I trade to win.

— LARRY HITE

		5	1		8			7
8	1		7	4				5
		4	9		6		2	
				1	2		4	9
						5	3	
9		4	5	3				2
	5		2		1			4
	2		4		7	5		
		7		5		8		

79

22

The saving man becomes the free man.

— CHINESE PROVERB

			8				9	1
			1		5			2
	6	9	2		7	3		8
4		3	9	8	6	1		7
	8			1	5			
7				2			6	
3		2	6			9	1	5
			8	5		7	2	
					2	4		6

80

23

When I was young, I thought money was the most important thing in life. Now that I'm old – I know it is.

— OSCAR WILDE

5	4	7						
6				1		5		7
	9	1	4	7		6	2	
3	6	4	8	2	1	7	5	
					7	3		4
		9		4	3	1		2
	3	5			2	9	7	
		6	7	8				5
9		8		5	4	2	1	

81

24

The price pattern reminds you that every movement of importance is but a repetition of similar price movements. As soon as you familiarize yourself with the actions of the past, you will be able to anticipate and act profitably upon forthcoming movements.

— JESSE LIVERMORE

	7	9	3					
3		4	1			2		
		8	9				3	5
		7	5	9		6	4	1
9			6		1			2
4		6			2			
		3		5				
		1		6	8	3	7	9
6		2	3	7				

82

25

If stock market experts were so expert, they would be buying stock, not selling advice.

— NORMAN RALPH AUGUSTINE

				5		1			8	7	
	4	1				8					5
			7				2	5	3		1
		2				1					
	3	4				6		7		9	
			8			5	9	2		3	
					6	2	5		4	1	
	5	9					4	1	7		
						7		8	2		9

83

26

Whenever I enter a position, I have a predetermined stop. That is the only way I can sleep. I know where I'm getting out before I get in. The position size on a trade is determined by the stop, and the stop is determined on a technical basis.

— BRUCE KOVNER

		5	1	2	9	4		8
2	9	1					6	7
3				6	7	1	2	9
						7	5	
4	3				6			
	7	5	9	1				
	1		4	3				5
			6				9	1
		6	2	9	1	3	8	

84

27

I am having an out of money experience.

— UNKNOWN

	8					1		
		9	1				5	
	1		8					
				8	2	7	4	
	5	7	4	2		9		
	2					8		
7		9		6	3	5	8	
1			3	5			7	
8			7	4	1		9	

85

28

What seems too high and risky to the majority generally goes higher and what seems low and cheap generally goes lower.

— WILLIAM O'NEIL

1	2			8		5		7
9	4	8				1		3
	7	5				9	4	8
			9	4	8			
8	9		6			3		
	6	7	2		1	8	9	
	5	6	1	2	3	8		
		1	8	9	4		7	5
	8							

86

29

Commodities tend to zig when the equity markets zag.

— JIM ROGERS

6	8				2			9
5	4	2	1	9	7			
1		7			8	2	5	4
		4		5				
7						4	2	6
3	1			6				
9		5	8	7		6	4	3
8	7	1	4					
4	3	6		2				7

87

30

If you find yourself in the bottom of a deep hole, the first thing to do is stop digging.

— WARREN BUFFETT

	9	7	5		3	1		8
5	6		8					2
8			2	9	7			5
3	2		4			8	9	7
	5		7		9			
			8	3		5		4
6				3		4	8	9
				9		7		
					2	3		

88

31

As a kid, I played Monopoly with the twist I invented of buying and selling shares in the bank. Well, today, I do the same.

— GEORGE SOROS

		8	3	5		4		1	
		4	5	7			2		3
9			7						
		6			7	9	3		
		9	4	1		2			
3	2		8	5			7	9	
		5		6				3	9
			6			3			2
		3					4	7	6

89

CARL ICAHN

Born in 1936 in Brooklyn, "tough-as-nails" investor Carl Celian Icahn was raised in a tough Queens neighborhood where he attended the Far Rockaway High School. An excellent student, his grades opened him the doors of Princeton University. There he graduated with a Bachelor of Arts in philosophy in 1957. Bowing to his parents' wishes, he enrolled in New York University School of Medicine. He hated every minute he spent there, leaving for good two years after.

In the meantime, foreshadowing his outstanding negotiation skills, Icahn revealed himself as an enormously talented poker player and earned substantial sums at the game.

In 1961 he joined Dreyfus & Co as a broker. He subsequently held jobs at Tessel, Petrick & Co. and Gruntal & Co.

In 1968, with the support and financial backing from his uncle Elliot Schnall, he bought a seat on the NYSE (New York Stock Exchange) and launched Icahn & Co., a securities firm specialized in arbitrage and options trading.

Together with Victor Posner, Nelson Peltz, T. Boone Pickens, Kirk Kerkorian, Sir James Goldsmith, and Saul Steinberg, Icahn belonged to the hall of fame of the notorious corporate raiders of the 1980s. He made millions for himself with hostile takeovers1[1], greenmail[2], and leveraged buy-outs[3], and at the same made money for the ordinary stockholders of the corporations he attacked. His ruthlessness and success were such that he is said to be the inspiration for the character Gordon Gekko in the 1987 movie *Wall Street*.

Icahn continues to this day to make regular headlines in the financial press with interventions in high-profile companies such as eBay, Apple, Herbalife, and Xerox.

He has made significant philanthropic donations, among them bestowing $200 million to the Mount Sinai School of Medicine.

---

1. The acquisition of a corporation by going directly to the company's shareholders or replacing its management to get the purchase approved.
2. Greenmail consists in buying a large number of shares in a company to threaten a hostile takeover with the aim that it offers to repurchase its shares at a premium.
3. Buying a publicly traded company using debt, often junk-bonds.

1

There is no pride like that of a beggar grown rich.

— FRENCH PROVERB

		8	9	4	3	5		2	
4									
				9	6			5	4
1		7				6	4		5
9				5	4		2		1
		3			1	2		6	8
8						4	1		
	5				7	1		9	6
				6		9	5		

90

2

The time to buy is when there's blood on the streets.

— SIR NATHAN MEYER ROTHSCHILD

		3				5		8
		2	8		9	1	3	4
		5						7
			9	8				
5		8	4		3			6
					6	8	5	
1	3	4	6	7	2	9		
7	2	6			8		4	1
			9	3				

92

3

I'm involved in the stock market, which is fun and, sometimes, very painful.

— REGIS PHILBIN

	1		7			6	3	
	6			2	4	3	1	9	7
		2				1		8	
				6					8
			9	3					
4	3						5	6	9
9	5			4			2		
		4	6				2	9	
			3	5	1			4	

93

4

Teacher: Billy, if you had 5$ and you asked your father for 3$ more, how many dollars would you have?
Billy: I would have five dollars...
Teacher: You don't know your arithmetic, Billy
Billy: You don't know my father, Mrs. Mutch...

— UNKNOWN

CARL ICAHN

7		6	3		1		8	
3						7	4	
	8				6			1
5	2		6	7		1		4
6		8		3		5	2	
	3		5		9		7	8
4		7	9	5				2
			8	6		4		
			2		1			3

94

5

What will the stock market will do? It will fluctuate!

— J.P. MORGAN

```
6 9 . | . 5 . | . 1 .
. . 4 | 8 . . | 7 . .
1 . 8 | 7 6 . | 4 5 3
------+-------+------
7 . 3 | 2 . 1 | . . .
. 1 . | . . 6 | . 7 .
8 . . | . 3 . | . . 1
------+-------+------
. 7 5 | 1 3 . | 6 . 8
3 4 1 | 6 . . | . 9 .
. . . | . 9 7 | 1 3 .
```

95

6

When you're in a losing streak, your ability to properly assimilate and analyze information is distorted because your confidence becomes impaired. You have to work very hard to restore that confidence, and cutting back trading size helps achieve that goal.

— BILL LIPSCHUTZ

			4		6	5		1	
5	2				1	8			7
		9			4			6	
		9		3	4	7	2	6	
	8	3							1
					1		3	4	
3	1						5	9	
2	4	7	6			1			
				8		4	7		

96

7

Money frees you from doing things you dislike. Since I dislike doing nearly everything, money is handy.

— GROUCHO MARX

	5		2		7		4	1
7		8	4			3	5	9
	4	1		9		7	2	8
	6		3	4	9	8		
9	3			5		1	6	
8	7		6	2	1			4
5	8	3				4		6
		7	9	6		5		

97

8

I always laugh at people who say "I've never met a rich technician." I love that! It is such an arrogant, nonsensical response. I used fundamentals for nine years and got rich as a technician.

— MARTY SCHWARTZ

8			3	2	1	4		
			6		7	9		
		4	5			2	1	
3			7			8	9	
7			9			3		1
		9	1	3	2	6		7
9	5	8	2	1			6	
	3			7	6	5		
								2

98

9

In life and business, there are two cardinal sins. The first is to act precipitously without thought and the second is to not act at all.

— CARL ICAHN

6				3		8	2	5
4							9	
8	2			7	6	1		3
5		2		9	7		1	
7	6		4		1			
		3			8	7	6	9
	7					2	5	8
3			8			9	7	
	5	8	7				3	1

99

10

The relation between the stock market and the economy is like a man walking his dog. It is tough to determine the direction of the dog which will get easily distracted.

The dog will sometimes sprint ahead, lag or just run around randomly but over time both the dog and the owner will get to the same place. While the owner walks 1 km, the dog runs 3 to 4 times that. The dog is the stock market, and the owner is the economy.

— ANDRÉ KOSTOLANY

				2	6		4	7		5		
						3				6	1	
					3	6	1	2	8			7
6			2					1		3	4	
	1				9				2	6		
		4				6			7	8		
9					5		3		1			
					1	7						
7		6				9						

187

11

He that is afraid of the devil does not grow rich.

— ITALIAN PROVERB

	8	6			4			7
			7		5			
	7	9			3	1		
9					6		1	
6	5	8			1	7	9	
	3						6	
7		4	9	5				6
8		5		3		4	7	1
2		3	1			5	8	9

100

12

I owe much; I have nothing; the rest I leave to the poor.

— FRANÇOIS RABELAIS

			4			9	5	
		4				7		
5		9			6			4
			6		7		8	1
						3	9	
	8					2		
1		8	9	5			2	7
3		5	7	6			4	8
6	2	7	4		1	5		

101

13

Experience is what you get when you don't get what you want.

— HOWARD MARKS

3	8	6	9		2	7		
	9			7				
		7	6	3	8	1		
			8	6				2
	3					4	7	
1		9	4	7	5		6	3
			5			3	8	6
			4	3		6		1
			3	1	2			

102

14

Amateurs want to be right. Professionals want to make money.

— ALAN GREENSPAN

4		1	7		2	6	8	
							9	
				4				7
	5	6		1		7		2
		9			3			8
	7	3		8	5	1		
9		4						
	2	7				1		
6		5	4	9	1		7	3

103

15

Markets to move from relative lows to relative highs and vice versa every two to four days. After several days of a market rally, everyone wants to buy it, and I sell. Conversely, when the market has been down for a few days, and everyone is bearish, I buy.

— JACK SCHWAGER

	4	2		8	7			
	8		1			2		4
	1							
2	6				8	1		9
		8		1		4	2	6
3	9	1		6		8		
8		5	3		1	6	4	2
1							5	
	2	6			5	9		3

104

16

There is a new income tax form.
    Line 1 says: "How much did you make last year?"
    Line 2 says: "How much do you have left?"
    Line 3 says: "Send it to us."

— UNKNOWN

				7		5				9	
4	3					9	8		6		
				9						3	
2				7		5			9		1
5	6	3		1							
				7			8				
7							2		1		4
3	2					4			5	7	9
1	5	4							9	3	2	6

105

17

Writing down your trades is the best exercise in the world.

— LINDA BRADFORD RASCHKE

	2	5				6	1	
	4		1	9				
			7	2	5		3	4
	3			1		7	2	
6			5		2	4		
	7			4		9		1
9						4		
2	5	7	8	3	4		9	6
4		3			1	5	7	

106

18

I think gold is a great thing to sew into your garments if you're a Jewish family in Vienna in 1939 but I think civilized people don't buy gold.

— CHARLIE MUNGER

8				4		3		
3	4			2		8		5
2	6				8			4
		6			5	4	9	3
5	8					1		
9		4			2		8	
			9		4		1	2
		3		6	1			8
		2	5			3		9

107

19

As an investor my job is to figure out what will happen rather than what should happen.

— DAVID EINHORN

7				6			8	
				9		3	4	7
9	8		3		7	1		
	9		7		4	2	6	1
4	7	3		2	6		9	
		9				1		
3	4	7	6	1		8		9
6	1		8		9	4		

108

20

What feels good is often the wrong thing to do.

— WILLIAM ECKHARDT

		9	3		1			
	5		2		6	9		7
8	6	2		4		3	5	1
1	3				8		9	4
2	8	6	7	9	4			5
		7		3	5			
	1	3				4		
					9			3
			5	1		2		

109

21

When money speaks, the truth keeps silent.

— RUSSIAN PROVERB

			8	7	1		3	
				1			5	8
	6			5	8	1		
			7	3	2		8	5
				9	5			
			5	4		2		3
				6		9	4	7	1
	5		9	1		7		2	6
		1			3	2	5	8	9

110

22

If you have an approach that makes money, then money management can make the difference between success and failure... ... I try to be conservative in my risk management. I want to make sure I'll be around to play tomorrow. Risk control is essential.

— MONROE TROUT

				7	2	9	5		8	
		9		4				6	1	
		5						7	2	
	7				4				6	
				3					7	
	6	8			7	1		5		
1					5	7		8	3	
	5	7								
8							7	2		

111

23

Dogs have no money. Isn't that amazing? They're broke their entire lives. But they get through. You know why dogs have no money?... No Pockets.

— JERRY SEINFELD

4	6	8		2			1	7
5		2			9		6	
9		7		8			3	
		6			7	8		
7		3						6
		4	5	6	2	7		
1	8		2	4	6	3	7	
6	2	4		5				
						6	2	

112

24

Wall Street's graveyards are filled with men who were right too soon.

— WILLIAM HAMILTON

			3			1		5	
			4	8	5	7	2	9	3
	5				9			1	4
8				2	9		4		1
3		9		1			7	8	
4	6	1			8		3	2	
		8		9	3	2	1		6
9		2		6		4	5	7	8
	4								2

113

25

The point is ladies and gentlemen that greed, for lack of a better word, is good.

— GORDON GEKKO (WALL STREET)

		8				5	3	7	2
9									1
	7	2		1	6			4	9
				7					
2	3				1		9	5	
			6	5	4		2		
6				9		4		2	3
	4			3		2	8	1	
	2	3			8	1	4		5

114

26

You have to decide ahead of time how much of a drawdown would imply that the system is not as good as you thought it was, and therefore shouldn't be traded.

— EDWARD THORP

7		2	1				5	
6		1			8	2		
		9	4			6	3	
			8	5			2	7
	8				2		6	
						9	8	
5							1	6
4	2	7	6	3				8
3		6			5			2

115

27

Every day, self-proclaimed stock market "experts" tell us why the market just went up or down, as if they really knew. So where were they yesterday?

— UNKNOWN

28

All a company report and balance sheet can tell you is the past and the present. They cannot tell future.

— NICOLAS DARVAS

29

When the public is most frightened, only the strong are left, and that's when the market is in the best possible hands.

— VICTOR NIEDERHOFFER

		8					4	6
			2	7	6	1		
2	7	6			1		3	5
		2	4	9			6	3
		9	6	3	7		1	
		3		2	8		4	
			7			2		
		3			2	9	5	1
			5	1				

118

30

Money can't buy you happiness, but it does bring you a more pleasant form of misery.

— SPIKE MILLIGAN

		9	4			7	5	
	4		7			9	6	3
		7	3	9				
9	6	3					7	5
				2		3		
7	5	2	6			1	4	
	8		5	2				9
2	7			9	6			
3		6	8					7

119

JAMES (JIM) CHANOS

Jim Chanos graduated from Yale University in 1980 with a degree in Economics and Political Science. Perhaps the US best-known short-seller[1], he founded and is the managing partner of Kynikos Associates LP.[2] Chanos is often invited to comment on financial news shows.

Chanos modus operandi is almost the mirror image from the one of Warren Buffet. Both do in-depth research looking for companies whose stock is mispriced, but while Buffet focus is finding undervalued companies to buy, Chanos searches for those with inflated valuations to sell.

His first big coup was Baldwin-United, a company that started by selling pianos and that by a series of acquisitions had become an insurance giant and one of Wall Street's most touted stocks.

Chanos smelled fraud in the company's accounts, and it eventually went bankrupt, proving him right.

Chanos list of successes includes big wins on Tyco, WorldCom, and several subprime-mortgage lenders. His most significant moment of fame came when he predicted the fall of Enron Corp. and kept on increasing its short position as more and more information about the company hit the news.

Today, one of his largest short positions is Tesla. He thinks that Tesla's equity is worthless, that the company makes self-serving announcements, and that Elon Musk will eventually leave Tesla to work in SpaceX. A lot of people are convinced that the Twitter handle Diogenes, a frequented tweeter on Elon Musk and Tesla is Chanos.

Jim Chanos lectures on the history of financial fraud at the Yale School of Management and the University of Wisconsin Business School.

---

1. A short seller profits if the price of a share declines. The short seller opens a position by selling stock, expecting to repurchase it later at a lower price and keep the difference.
2. Kynikos is the Greek word for "cynic." Chanos is of Greek ancestry. His family ran a chain of dry-cleaning shops in Milwaukee.

1

Interest on debt grows without rain.

— JEWISH PROVERB

9				6		5		
4		6	5		8		2	9
8	5			2			6	4
				7		1		
			8			9	5	
3	8	1	9	5	2			
5	2		6					1
7	6				1	2	8	5
1	3	4	2			6		7

120

2

A billion here, a billion there, and pretty soon you're talking about real money.

— EVERETT DIRKSEN

			6	5	4		8	
4				5	1			2
			7	6	2	5	4	9
	3	1				6	9	
6						4		3
	4		3	1			7	
	6		4	9	5	3	1	8
9	5		8		1			7
1	8							5

121

3

Greed is all right, by the way I think greed is healthy. You can be greedy and still feel good about yourself.

— IVAN BOESKY

3	1						9	
			6	9		7		
	8	6		3	1	4	2	
			1	6	3	5	7	
		1				8	4	
7	2		8		9	1		3
8			2	1		9		
	7		9	5	4	3	8	6
5					6			

4

The secret to investing is to figure out the value of something - and then pay a lot less.

— JOEL GREENBLATT

			9	5				
							3	
		4		2	1	9	5	
2			8			7	4	
8	9	5	4	6		2	1	3
		6			2	8	9	5
				4	6			
7		6			3			9
		1				6	7	4

123

5

Investing is a business where you can look very silly for a long period of time before you are proven right.

— BILL ACKMAN

2				3	1			7
			8		5	2	4	9
	5			2	4			6
9	4		6	3	7			
				7		9	2	
	5		9					
	2	3			6	8		5
1				5	8	4		2
8			2	4	9		6	

124

6

The psychologist Gerd Gigerenzer has a simple heuristic. Never ask the doctor what you should do. Ask him what he would do if he were in your place. You would be surprised at the difference.

— NASSIM TALEB

4	7	6	1		5	2	8	
	5				2	8		
2	8				7		1	
	2				4	7		
	4		5			9		
		5			9	2	4	6
	6				5	1	9	
5	1		2	8				
					4		3	

125

7

A long-term investment is a short term investment that failed.

— UNKNOWN

	3	4				1	9	
5				8	1	2		
1			2		4		5	6
8		9	4		3	6	7	5
							1	9
7			1		8	4		
9	8			4	2			
		2	6			9	8	
		5	8			3	4	2

126

8

Don't be a hero. Don't have an ego. Always question yourself and your ability. Don't ever feel that you are very good. The second you do, you are dead.

— PAUL TUDOR JONES

1	9				6	4	2	
6	3			4	2	1		8
		5	9			6		
	4	2				7	6	
						5	4	
7		3	2			1	9	
9			7	6	3	5		
3	7	6	4	2				1
				1		3		

127

9

If past history was all there was to the game, the richest people would be librarians.

— WARREN BUFFETT

6	1	2	9	8	3			
9			5					2
			6			3	9	8
4		5			1			9
	6					4		5
3			7		4			1
	4			2	6	8		
	2						4	7
			4	7			2	6

128

10

In the history of the world, no one has ever washed a rented car.

— LAWRENCE SUMMERS

8		2	5	1		7	4	
				6				
4	6						1	9
	4			8				1
2	8		1			4		
1	9	5		7				
	2	8	5	1	9		4	
5	1	9		6		3	2	8
		4		3				5

129

11

Public money is like holy water; everyone helps himself to it.

— ITALIAN PROVERB

	2	8						
1			5		7	2	8	
		9	3			4		1
	5			3				6
		9	6	1		5	4	7
6	1	2	7				9	
9				6	3	7		4
				7	1	8		9
	7	1		8			3	2

130

12

Jesus saves. But wouldn't it have been better if he had invested?

— UNKNOWN

			2	9	1		4	
6				4	8	6		
	4	8		3	5			
8	6	3	5		9		7	4
5		9		7				
		4		6				9
	5				7	4	8	
	1	7		8	6			2
	8	6		5	2		1	7

131

13

A lot of people would rather understand the market than make money.

— ED SEYKOTA

14

People who lose money always need someone to blame.

— JAMES CHANOS

			2	8	3	7		5		4		
								9		2	8	
						2	8			7	6	
								4		3		
	9					3			6			
		2	8		5	7	6			1		
			9							7	6	
					6	5	7			9		
					4		1	2			3	

133

15

The way to build superior long-term returns is through preservation of capital and home runs...When you have tremendous conviction on a trade, you have to go for the jugular. It takes courage to be a pig.

— STANLEY DRUCKENMILLER

				5	8	1		9	
			5				7		6
						7		1	
6				1			4		9
5	7	1		9					
4				3		2	5		
			7	8	9	5	3	4	
9				2					
3	4	2	7		6		5		

134

16

I just made a killing in the stock market -- I shot my broker.

— HENNY YOUNGMAN

		6		2	9			3
	7	2	8					
3			6	5	1	2		7
					5			9
	5		9	7				4
	9			8	4		6	
7	2	9		3	8	5	1	
			5	1				2
		5		9			3	8

135

17

When the weather changes, nobody believes the laws of physics have changed. Similarly, I don't believe that when the stock market goes into terrible gyrations its rules have changed.

— BENOIT MANDELBROT

4	6	7	3	5		8		
	9			1	8	2		
	2			4			3	5
1	8	9	2		4		3	
7		2				9		
3			9	1	8		7	4
2	7					5		
	3	4						
		1		8		4	6	3

136

18

Two traders are walking uptown from Wall Street to the subway. A mugger approaches them with a gun and demands all money. The one trader turns to the other and says, "Oh, by the way, here's the $100 I owe you..."

— UNKNOWN

	9						6	
7		8						9
6	5	1		2	9		7	
	2					9		
		5	9	3	6		8	2
		9			2	5		7
		7		9	1	2		3
	1		2			7	5	8
		2	7	5	8			1

137

19

One evening, while having dinner with a fundamentalist, I accidentally knocked a sharp knife off the edge of the table.

HUBARATO SAIKARO

He watched the knife twirl through the air, as it came to rest with the pointed end sticking into his shoe. Why didn't you move your foot? I exclaimed. I was waiting for it to come back up, he replied.

— ED SEYKOTA

				3				6
3		8		6	2	7		9
4		6		9	7	5	3	
		8		4			2	
				1		8		3
	1						5	
			3	5		1		
8			4	6	2		9	
			9	7	3	4		5

255

20

Some traders still think that a computer could not trade as well as they can.

— THOMAS PETERFFY

		7					8	2
6	3	5		2	9		4	7
			1					3
7			5					
	6		9		2			
2	9	8			4			6
	5	6	2	9	8		7	1
		9	4	7				5
			3	5	6		2	

138

21

There are good bets and bad bets, bets that you win, and bets that you lose. Winning a bad bet can be the most dangerous outcome of all because a success of that kind can encourage you to take more bad bets in the future, when the odds will be running against you.

— LARRY HITE

						8		1
5	9		4		8	6		
		4	2		7	9	3	5
	6	7				9	8	4
		9	8			2		7
4	1			2	6		9	
9	3				4		2	6
8	4		6			3		9
			9	3		4		

139

22

A man without money is like a wolf without teeth.

— FRENCH PROVERB

		9				5	7	1
3	2		1	5	7	9	4	
		7	8	9				
7	3		4	1	9		2	
4	1					3	5	
	8	2	7	3			9	
		1				6	3	5
2				6	3	7	1	9
5				7	1			2

140

23

Money is not the most important thing in the world. Love is. Fortunately, I love money.

— JACKIE MASON

3		4			1			
	2		6	7				4
8			3	9			5	
		2			7	4		9
	8	6			9	2		5
			1	5		7	8	
2				8		4		
6	7			4		5	2	
9		3	2				7	8

141

24

Mother: Why did you just swallow the money I gave you?
Son: Well, you did say it was my lunch money!

— UNKNOWN

5		1	7	6	3	4		2
	6	3				8		
				5	8			3
		8				2	4	9
				4			8	
9	2	4		5	8		7	
		5		3		9	2	
6						1	5	
4			8	1	5			

142

25

The key to making money in stocks is not to get scared out of them.

— PETER LYNCH

2	7		9	5				
	9	5				6		
	8	3	7		2	9		
				9	3	2		
	6	9		8		4		5
		8	4	7		6		
	1					3		9
				4		1		
9	3				8	5		7

143

26

In the short run, the market is a voting machine, but in the long run it is a weighing machine.

— BENJAMIN GRAHAM

5				9			4	6
		9				6		5
6	3			1	5			
2	5	9	8			1		
		3	6				9	2
					2	3	4	
1				7		9		3
9	7	5		8				1
3	2					5		

144

27

When the market goes against you, you hope that every bad day will be the last one and you lose more than you should have. When the market goes your way, you fear to lose your profit, and you get out too soon. Fight these two deep-seated instincts.

— JESSE LIVERMORE

		9				4		
		5	3	4		6		
8			9		6	5		
7		9		2		8		4
		5	8	3	4	7		9
		8			7		5	
5	2	1			3			6
						2		
9			1		2	4		

145

28

Madoff behind bars: Day One

Prison roommate: Let me get this straight, I give you one cigarette and next week you give me ten?

Madoff: It's that simple!

— UNKNOWN

8			1	4	5		9	
5	1						6	
3	9							4
		6		1	4			
4	8	1	5	9	7			6
7				3		4	8	
1	2	8	4	5	9	6		
9				7			2	8
			3			1	9	

146

29

Money is like manure. You have to spread it around or it smells.

— JOHN PAUL GETTY

		6	2					
8		2		5	4	6	3	
7	5		3		6		9	
			4	7		1		
	7	5				2	8	9
3	1							4
		7				9		8
6					2	4		5
		2	5	4				

147

30

People are living longer than ever before, a phenomenon undoubtedly made necessary by the 30-year mortgage.

— DOUG LARSON

			6	2	9		5	
2				5			8	
3		9	1		8		2	4
6					5		7	8
9		5	8		7			2
	1			4		5		3
7		1	6					
	6				9	3	8		7
5		3	7	8	1	2		

148

31

People who confuse what they wish were true with what is really true create distorted pictures of reality that make it impossible for them to make the best choices.

— RAY DALIO

			8	9	3		7	
9	3			1		4		
1	7	4	6		8		3	
			2				1	3
	9				1	8	6	
	1	3	8				9	
				2	6			
			3	4				
3	4		7				2	

149

RAYMOND (RAY) DALIO

Hedge fund billionaire Ray Dalio, born 1949 in Jackson Heights, New York City, the son of a jazz musician father and a homemaker mum, is currently on the list of 100 wealthiest people in the world.

After receiving a bachelor's degree in finance from Long Island University and an MBA from Harvard Business School Dalio traded commodity futures on the floor of the New York Stock Exchange. He worked at Dominick & Dominick and Shearson Hayden Stone, and in 1975 he founded investment management firm, Bridgewater Associates, right out of his apartment. Today the firm ranks as the world's #1 hedge fund by assets under management.

Dalio is a macro trader, developing thesis on broad issues such as G.D.P. growth, inflationary pressures, commodities, credit and currency exchanges that he then translates into specific investment strategies.

He is a great admirer of the late historian Will Durant's work, namely his "The Lessons of History." Dalio, who predicted the global financial crisis, has authored the script of the viral 31-minute video "How the Economic Machine Works; A Template for Understanding What is Happening Now," where he lays out his framework for interpreting the economy.

He also wrote "Principles," in which he elaborates on his investment and corporate management philosophy. Every employee at Bridgewater Associates has a copy of this book. It contains 210 lessons, among them:

- Make truth you #1 value.
- Failing is okay if you learn a lesson.
- Speak frankly and ask others to speak frankly to you.
- Persist until you reach your objective.
- Identify what you don't know.
- Keep risks low.
- Pareto[1] rules! 20% of the inputs cause 80% of the outputs.

Most recently Dalio authored "Principles for Navigating Big Debt Crises" which is free to download from his company website.

He and his wife have committed to *The Giving Pledge*.[2]

---

1. Vilfredo Pareto (1848 – 1923), Italian sociologist.
2. A campaign that encourages wealthy people to contribute a substantial part of their wealth to philanthropy.

1

Most people work just hard enough not to get fired and get paid just enough money not to quit.

— GEORGE CARLIN

2	1						3	
4	8		5	9	3	1	6	
		3	2	1		8		4
		4				2	1	6
			6		1			7
		1	8		4	5	9	
			1		2	7	4	
1	6		4					
		7			5		2	1

150

2

October. This is one of the peculiarly dangerous months to speculate in stocks in. The others are July, January, September, April, November, May, March, June, December, August, and February.

— MARK TWAIN

2	5	9				6		
4	3	8				5		
		6				4	3	8
		4	7					
7	1				6	4		
	2	6	8	4				
5		2	3	7	4	6		
3		4			1	5		
6			5	8	2	3	7	4

151

3

The time of maximum pessimism is the best time to buy, and the time of maximum optimism is the best time to sell.

— JOHN TEMPLETON

				9		6		
	1	2						
8				5			1	
4		3		2				
		1				4		
		6		3			2	5
6	2	9	7	8		5		
3		8		5		9	6	2
1	4			9	6	8	3	7

152

4

The first loss is the best loss.

— JIM ROGERS

	9			5		2		6
5	7	3					9	
	4			8	9			
6		9	7	1				4
1		7				6	8	9
3	2	4				1		7
			5		1	7		
9	1							8
7		2				9		

153

5

Sell in May and go away; don't come back until St Leger day.

— UNKNOWN

5	6	7					3	1
	8	4			3			5
1	9	3	5					
	1	9					8	7
3	5			2	8			
	2					5	6	3
						4	1	8
6	7	2		4	1		5	
	4			3	5		2	6

154

6

Great investment opportunities come around when excellent companies are surrounded by unusual circumstances that cause the stock to be mispriced.

— WARREN BUFFETT

		9			2		1	3
		2	6	1		5		
			8		9	7		
1		6		8	5	2		4
9	8	5	2	7				
			3		1	8		
	2	7		3		9		5
6	1		5			4	2	
5	9			2	7	1	3	6

155

7

History demonstrates that participants in financial markets are susceptible to waves of optimism. Excessive optimism shows the seeds of its own reversal in the form of imbalances that tend to grow over time.

— ALAN GREENSPAN

6	2		4	3		7		1
5	4		1	7			2	9
		7		2	9	4		
3		4	1			6	2	
8	1	7			2		4	
9		2						
			2		6		5	4
2	9				4		1	
4	3	5				2		

156

8

Remember, it's the quality of your ideas not the quantity that will result in the big money.

— JOEL GREENBLATT

3							6	
				2			4	
2		7	8		4			
8				9	3	6		
9	3		6		5	4	8	2
			4		2	1	9	3
				6		4		
	9		2			3		
	7		3	1		5	6	9

157

9

You can be young without money, but you can't be old without it.

— TENNESSEE WILLIAMS

4	8		3	9			7	2
9	5	3	7	2	6			
2					4	5		
1				3				7
	9	8	5					1
7		5		1	4			
			9				2	6
	7	9	2	6		3		
			4	8		9		

158

10

My mother liked to save wherever possible, so she avoided dry-cleaning. Proud of her savings, she boasted to my father, "Just think, Fred, we are five dollars richer because I washed this dress by hand."

"Good," my dad quickly replied. "Wash it again!"

— UNKNOWN

RAYMOND (RAY) DALIO

	5	3			1			
1					7			
7				3	4	1		
					9			2
	4	5		2	3			8
	1	2	7		6			5
8	9	4	3	1	5	2		
		1	6			2	8	9
2		7	9			5		

159

11

It's folly to live poor and die rich.

— SCOTTISH PROVERB

6		9		8	2		4	
2					5		6	7
5	3				7	8		
		7			8	5	3	
8		1	5	3	4			
4	5	3			6	1		
3	4	5		7	9		1	8
7	9	6	8					
			4					

160

12

I have always believed that a single talented analyst, working very hard, can cover an amazing amount of investment landscape, and this belief remains unchallenged in my mind.

— MICHAEL BURRY

	8	2	7	3	1		9	
	3	1	9	5				
9	5			8				7
	9		2				8	1
	6	5	1	7				4
	7		4		3			
3		7				1	6	
5							7	3
8		6	3	4	7		9	

161

13

Everything I have is for sale, except for my kids and possibly my wife.

— CARL ICAHN

			8			5	2	
6	5	9	3			4	8	7
	2			7	4		9	
3	7		5		6			9
		5	2				4	3
9		2		3	7			8
5		1	7	2		8		4
2				6		8		5
4	8					3		

162

14

If I could choose between world peace and a reasonable fortune, my first Lambo would be orange.

— @GSELEVATOR

	8		1				5		6
		2	9		6	5	1		3
			5	8				4	
		7						9	
	1	8	6	9		3	2		7
	9				7	2	6		8
	6								
	3	9	8		5	4	7	6	1
			4					3	

163

15

A Penny Saved is a Penny Earned.

— BENJAMIN FRANKLIN

9		5	4					6
8	2	4		3		5	9	1
3					9	2		
	3			1	5			
5		1	8					3
4	8	2	6	7		1		
	4		3				1	5
		3			1		8	2
	5		4					7

164

16

The concept of paying one-hundred-and-something times earnings for any company for me is just anathema. Having said that, at the end of the day, your job is to buy what goes up and to sell what goes down so really who gives a damn about PE's?

— PAUL TUDOR JONES

			4	6	5	9	8		3
6	5				3				4
				2					
		3	7		4	5	9	2	
							8		
	2	5			3	4	7		
			3	9	6	1	4	8	
9	6	4				2			
				7	2				

165

17

The ability to change one's mind is a key characteristic of the successful investor. Dogmatic and rigid personalities rarely succeed in the markets. Sustained investment success requires the ability to modify and even change strategies as markets evolve.

— JACK SCHWAGER

	9		3					5
			2	5		9		
	7							8
		1	3		2	4		
2	5	7	4	9	6			3
	4	9	1				7	2
				1	7	6		9
	2		6			3	8	
	6		8			2		7

166

18

Trade what you see, not what you think.

— UNKNOWN

					6	7		3
	6		1	7		8		2
				2	8	6		
		5	8					
8	9					3		
1		4		7	5	2	8	9
4	1	6		3				
5	3	7	2	8		4		6
		8				5	3	7

167

19

Don't look for the needle in the haystack. Just buy the haystack!

— JACK BOGLE

7	5	1					8	
9				4	6		1	7
4	6			7	5	2	3	
				1				
	7	6	5			4		
						7	6	1
		4	7	5		8		2
5				9	8	1	4	6
2					1	3		

168

20

Money is better than poverty, if only for financial reasons.

— WOODY ALLEN

8	2	1	4	6			9	
			3	5		1	8	
				2				
	8	2	7		6		5	9
7	4	6	9	3	5			
				8	2			7
		8		7				5
		4	5				2	
				1	8	7		6

169

21

No amount of money can make others speak well of you behind your back.

— CHINESE PROVERB

9				2		5	6	
7		1	8		6	4		
	5		9	4	3			
			3					1
3			1			4		
1		5	6			2		
5	9				7	8	2	
	7			1		6		
	8	5	6	9			4	

170

22

Every decade has its characteristic folly, but the basic cause is the same: people persist in believing that what has happened in the recent past will go on happening into the indefinite future, even while the ground is shifting under their feet.

— GEORGE J. CHURCH

2		5			4		7	
4						3		2
7					5	4		
	7	6						
	2		4		8	7		9
	4	1				2		5
3			2	8	4	1	9	6
1	8				6	9	2	3
6	9			2	3			

171

23

You think the 'True Little Me' is entitled to do what it wants to do. And, for instance, why shouldn't the True Little Me overspend my income.

There once was a man who became the most famous composer in the world but was utterly miserable most of the time, and one of the reasons was because he always overspent his income.

That was Mozart.

If Mozart can't get by with this kind of asinine conduct, I don't think you should try.

— CHARLIE MUNGER

2	6					7	4	
3			4	9	7		8	2
7		9		2	6			
1			7	4		2	6	8
9	7		6	8			5	
8								4
			1	3	5	4	9	7
5		3						
	9	7		6				5

177

24

The financial markets generally are unpredictable. So that one must have different scenarios... The idea that you can predict what's going to happen contradicts my way of looking at the market.

— GEORGE SOROS

			5	1			2	
5		8	9	2		6	7	
			4	6				8
7	4		8					
8				9			6	7
2	3		7		6		5	1
6		4	1	8	5			
				3				6
					4		8	5

172

25

In bear markets, stocks usually open strong and close weak. In bull markets, they tend to open weak and close strong.

— WILLIAM J. O'NEILL

			6			
7		5	3			
			1	6	8	7
8		9	5	1	3	
9		2	1		4	8
2		8	7		6	9
3	2	4			7	6
	8			2		3
6		3		8		4

173

26

It's much easier to learn what you should do in trading than to do it. Good systems tend to violate normal human tendencies.

— WILLIAM ECKHARDT

174

27

Make sure you have an edge. Know what your edge is. And have rigid risk control rules.

— MONROE TROUT

7		1	3	8				4
	3	8		4		7		1
			1	7	5			8
1	5	3		6	8			
		6	7	9	4			3
				3		8	2	6
9	1	5			3	6	4	7
3				7				5
6	4			5		3		

176

28

Every morning in Africa, a gazelle wakes up.
 It knows it must outrun the fastest lion or it will be killed.

Every morning in Africa, a lion wakes up. It knows it must run faster than the slowest gazelle, or it will starve.

It doesn't matter whether you're the lion or a gazelle-when the sun comes up, you'd better be running.

— AFRICAN PROVERB

2					1		7
	9	6		1	8	2	
4	7	1		8	6		9
8		5			7		
6	2	9		3	5		
	3	7		5			
5		4				7	6
	8	2	7	6		5	
		3	5		4	9	

270

29

All I ask is the chance to prove that money can't make me happy.

— SPIKE MILLIGAN

			1	9		2	5	
6		9		8	2	3		
	8		4			9		1
			2	5				7
2				7		3	9	
7	4	3	6	1			2	
			8			7		
8				3	4			9
3	7	4				5	8	2

178

30

The market may be bad, but I slept like a baby last night. I woke up every hour and cried.

— UNKNOWN

	9	1					8	6
	7	5	8		3	9		
3		6	9		4			
5		8	4			2		
6		9						8
		7	3	8				
	1			5		8		
7		3	6	4		9		2
8				2				3

179

NICHOLAS DARVAS

Nicholas Darvas was a dancer, self-taught investor, and author. Born in Hungary in 1920, he studied economics at the University of Budapest. In 1943, using a forged exit visa, he fled to Istanbul with only a few pounds sterling on his pocket. Sometime later he met his half-sister Julia, and partner with her to make a living as a ballroom-dancer couple.

The two emigrated to the US in 1951 where they became the country's highest-paid ballroom dancing pair. Their success led to a row of world tours.

Darvas interest in trading started when a Toronto nightclub owner, who could not pay Darvas in cash, gave him instead three thousand shares of Brilund, a Canadian mining company. Two months later, the stock tripled, and he began an intense study of the stock market.

When not performing, Nicolas spent most of the time reading books about trading in the stock market. Two books he carried everywhere he went: "Tape Reading and Market Statistic," by Humphrey Bancroft Neill and "The Battle for Surviving of Investment" by Gerald M. Loeb. He said he read from them every single day.

He developed a trading method that came to be known as "Darvas Box Theory." It combines momentum with technical analysis to determine when to enter and exit the market. Darvas supposedly turned a $10,000 investment into $2 million over 18 months using this method.

In May 1959, Time Magazine devoted almost a full page in its Business section his story and trading technique.

The New York Attorney General was not convinced and in 1960 and stated that his story was "unqualifiedly false" and that he could find "ascertainable" profits of only $216,000. The probe was blocked by the court, which ruled that the investigation was an "unwarranted invasion of the free press."

Darvas is the author of "How I Made 2.000.000,00 in Stock Market". Published in 1960, it is a perennial bestseller. His other titles are "Wall Street: The other Las Vegas "(1964), "The Anatomy of Success" (1965), "The Darvas System for Over-the-Counter Profits" (1971), and "You can still make it in the Market"(1977).

He reportedly died in 1977.

1

Many a pupil has gained more wealth than his master.

— GREEK PROVERB

					3	2		
	4	6		8			7	1
	8	2	9	1				
				7		2		5	3
		1	2	3	4	5		
3				9			1		7
5				6			7		
					7	8			
			8	5			9		6

180

2

The main purpose of the stock market is to make fools of as many men as possible.

— BERNARD BARUCH

8	4	5				2	3	7
			2	3	7			
			8		5	9	1	6
		4		9		6	2	
5	9	1	6		3	7	8	
			7				9	
1			3					
	7		4	5	9	1		
4		9		6	2	3		

181

3

The stock market is filled with individuals who know the price of everything, but the value of nothing.

— PHILIP FISHER

						1	5	7
	8					1	5	7
				5				6
	7				6	2	4	
	4	9	5	7		6		
	5				3			4
3			9		4	7		5
	2	4			7		6	
7	1		3	6				
	3		4		2	5		1

182

4

Buying gold is just buying a put against the idiocy of the political cycle. It's that simple!

— KYLE BASS

8	2				9	4		
		7		3				
	4		2				9	7
3		4	8	2	5			
5		2	9	7		3		
7		9	1	4				8
	3	1	5			9		
			6			4		1
9	7				4			

184

5

There is no such thing as a no sale call. A sale is made on every call you make. Either you sell the client some stock or he sells you a reason he can't. Either way a sale is made, the only question is who is gonna close? You or him? Now be relentless, that's it, I'm done.

— JIM YOUNG (BOILER ROOM)

				5		9	2	1			6	
						6	3	8		7		
6	3						5		2	1	9	
1	4	2										
	9	3				6	5		4	2	1	
7	6	5				4				3		
2		4		3								
3	1			5			6	7				
				7								

185

6

Things always become obvious after the fact.

— NASSIM TALEB

	5	1		4	8	9		7
		6	9		7			
9	3	7				8	6	
		3	2					
1		5			4		9	
4		6			3	5	1	2
			5	1			4	
5					6		7	
6	4	8	3			2	5	1

186

7

Money is like a sixth sense – and you can't make use of the other five without it.

— WILLIAM SOMERSET MAUGHAM

				6				
5				8		9		3
	2	8		9				4
8	1	4	7				6	5
9			5			4		1
				4	8			
	9	1		7		5	4	
3	6		8	5	4	1	2	
4			9	1			3	6

188

8

Price is what you pay. Value is what you get.

— WARREN BUFFETT

8	3	9		7		1	4	2
5						9		3
4		1	8		9			
9						2		
	8					3	9	4
1			9	4	3	7		
7	9	8			5		3	
		5	3		4		7	
	1	4	7		8			

183

9

Intaxication: Euphoria at getting a refund from the IRS, which lasts until you realize it was your money to start with.

— UNKNOWN

		2		6	5		9	
		1			7			
5		9			2			
			1		6	5		
						9		
3						8		
1	3	5	4				8	
7	9	4		2		1		5
2	8			1		7		

189

10

Only a fool tests the depth of the water with both feet.

— AFRICAN PROVERB

6		3	7			4	8	
				4	8		3	6
4	8		6		3	5	7	
7	9	5	8	2	4	6		
	4			6	1			
					9	2		8
		9	4		2		6	
8	2	4	1					5
1	3		9			8	2	

190

11

After spending many years in Wall Street and after making and losing millions of dollars I want to tell you this: It never was my thinking that made the big money for me. It always was my sitting.

— JESSE LIVERMORE

2			3			5		
				7	5			
	9	5	2			3		4
				9	6		2	
	9			4			8	
4	2		5	3				6
7	4			5	9	8	1	
	5	9	8	1	2		4	3
	1					6	5	9

191

12

Fortunes are made by buying low and selling too soon.

— SIR NATHAN MEYER ROTHSCHILD

4		9	8	6		1	5	3
		8	1	5			7	9
		3		4	7	8		2
		7	2	8				5
	6		3					7
3	1	5		9		8		
		3				2	8	
7	9		6			3	1	
		8		3				

192

13

The market can remain irrational longer than you can remain solvent.

— JOHN MAYNARD KEYNES

		5	4		2		1	8	9
	2			1					4
						4	2		
				7	5	6			
		5	3	6	2				8
6				9	1		4		
9	1						3		
			7	2			8	9	1
		6	2			1		4	7

193

14

I have two basic rules about winning in trading as well as in life:
 1 - If you don't bet, you can't win.
 2 - If you lose all your chips, you can't bet.

— LARRY HITE

3				8				
1	6				7	3		
	7						8	1
8		6	7		5		9	3
2		7			9	1		
9	3				8	7		5
		9	3	8		5		
		8		7		3	4	
		2		9	3	4		6

194

15

I've learned many things from George Soros, but perhaps the most significant is that it's not whether you're right or wrong that's important, but how much money you make when you're right and how much you lose when you're wrong.

— STANLEY DRUCKENMILLER

			7		8	9		5	
						6			7
					7				8
3					2	7		9	4
1		7			8				
8	9	4			6	5		7	1
			8		3	6	5	2	7
			3				7	4	
			1	2	9	4		5	3

195

16

Budgeting: a mathematical confirmation of your suspicions.

— A. A. LATIMER

```
              1 | 8
  2 1 9 | 7 3 8 | 4 5 6
        | 6 4   | 1 9
  ---------------------
  9 2 4 | 1   3 |   8
        | 8 5 6 |
  5 6 8 |       |     7
  ---------------------
  4 9   |     7 | 5   8
  1     |   8 5 |   6
        | 6   9 | 7   1
```

196

17

I believe that only short-term price swings can be predicted with any precision. The accuracy of a prediction drops off dramatically, the more distant the forecast time. I'm a strong believer in chaos theory.

— LINDA BRADFORD RASCHKE

197

18

Someone stole all my credit cards, but I won't be reporting it. The thief spends less than my wife did.

— HENNY YOUNGMAN

			3	1	8		2	7
	8	9						
		4			3	9	1	8
9		8	4			3		
	1	7	3			8	9	6
	2	5			8	7		1
8	3	6		9			5	4
7		1						3
5		2	8	3	6			

198

19

An economist is an expert who will know tomorrow why the things he predicted yesterday didn't happen today.

— UNKNOWN

			3	1	8		2	7
		8	9					
			4			3	9	1	8
9			8	4			3	
		1	7	3			8	9	6
		2	5			8	7		1
8	3	6		9			5	4
7		1						3
5		2		8	3	6		

199

20

The beggar is not afraid of the drawbacks of being rich.

— INDIAN PROVERB

2		1		8	9			
		8				2		
			1	2	7	9	4	
6	5		7			8		
1	2	7		4				
8					6			7
		9			3	7		2
3	6	5	2			4		
7		2	8			5		6

200

21

When you have a position, you put it on for a reason, and you've got to keep it until the reason no longer exists. Don't take profits just for the sake of taking profits. You have to have a strategy to trade, know how it works and follow through on it.

— RICHARD DENNIS

	7	3	8	5	2	1	4	9
8		2		1	4			6
9	1			7	3	5	2	
	8	1	3				5	2
		7			5			4
2		5			1	9		3
				4	9		6	5
	4	9			6	2		1
	3	6		2	8			

201

22

Every once in a while, the market does something so stupid it takes your breath away.

— JIM CRAMER

```
6 1     | 9 8  |
3   |8 4|   6  |
  9 8|6  |      
-----+---+------
  6 2|7  3|4 9  
     |9 8 4|   6
     |9 1  |  5 
-----+-----+----
  1 6|    5|8 4 9
7 5  |4 9 8|    1
     |4 2  |3    
```

202

23

The difference between playing the stock market and the horses is that one of the horses must win.

— JOEY ADAMS

3	2				9	8		
6	4		8	5		3		
8	5				1			9
	3	5	6	2		7	8	4
		2				1		
7	8					9		
			2					6
2		3						8
			5				9	3

203

24

It's not the mathematical skill that's critical to winning; it's the discipline of being able to stick to the system.

— BLAIR HULL

			3	7	4		9		6
	5	4	1		6				
	2		9			7	1		
		8	3	5		1	6	9	2
				9					7
					8	3		1	
	3		8	1	5	4	2	6	
		1					7		
	6	9		3	7			4	

204

25

Bumper sticker on Wall Street: My other Porsche is for sale.

— UNKNOWN

8					7	6	3	
4	2			3	9			1
	9			8				
1	8			4	2		9	6
	4			6			8	5
	3		5		8	4	2	
9	6	3		5		7		2
5	1		2		4	6		
		4		9	6	5		

205

26

Always understand the risk/reward of the trade as it now stands, not as it existed when you put the position on. Some people say, "I was only playing with the market's money." That's the most ridiculous thing I ever heard.

— BILL LIPSCHUTZ

			9			1	6	7
4	5	9					8	2
						5		4
6	7				2			9
		8			4	7		6
	4	5	7		6			8
	6	7				9	4	5
8	2		4	5	9		7	
		9				8		3

206

27

Our favorite holding period is forever.

— WARREN BUFFETT

7		3	4	5		6		
							8	3
6				8		5		
1		9		7	8	4	5	2
3		8						6
		5				3		8
2	4			9		8	3	7
9		6						5
8	3		5	2				

207

28

I spend my day trying to make myself as happy and relaxed as I can be. If I have positions going against me, I get right out; if they are going for me, I keep them.

— PAUL TUDOR JONES

			8	3		6		
8	3	5	9					
			1	2		8		5
			5		2		9	3
		2	4			7	1	
4				1		5		
6				5	1		4	8
	5	1		4		6	7	
		4		6	9		5	1

208

29

You can't predict. You can prepare.

— HOWARD MARKS

4	6	3			8			
		1				3	4	6
		9	4		3	7		
			3					7
3		6				9	5	
1		7						4
7		8				4	6	3
2	9		6					
6		4			7			

209

30

Economy is the wealth of the poor and the wisdom of the rich.

— FRENCH PROVERB

		7	2	5	8	4	3	9	
4									
		1		7	2		8	4	5
		9	7		5				
			5	4			7		
		4	1		7	2	5		6
			6			1	9	7	3
1			4		9			5	2
7			9	2	6	5			8

210

31

You get recessions, you have stock market declines. If you don't understand that's going to happen, then you're not ready, you won't do well in the markets.

— PETER LYNCH

			1	9	6	2	5	7
9								
		5		1		6	4	
7	2	5				9	6	
1		3				7		5
		9	6	2				
6	4	9	5	7				3
5		2		8	3	4	9	6
3	1				9		7	

211

JESSE LIVERMORE

Trading legend Jesse Lauriston Livermore, nicknamed *the boy plunger*, was born in 1877 in a poor farmer's family in rural Massachusetts. At fourteen years of age, he escaped to Boston, where he got a job posting stock quotes in a chalkboard at Paine Webber's brokerage.

He started betting on bucket shops[1] and made some money. He seemed to had a gift for it, and soon he left Paine Webber to bet full-time. His consistent winnings made him persona non grata at the bucket shops who promptly barred him.

He took his $10,000 of winning and went to Wall Street aiming to trade stocks. He soon went bust.

A fast learner, with a contrarian streak, he developed a set of beliefs that guided his trading. He advocated always trading with the trend and defended that prices were never too high to begin buying or too low to begin selling.

Some of the positions he took gave him an almost mythical aura as a trader. He opened a massive short position on Union Pacific stock on April 17, 1906. The following was the day of the great earthquake that almost destroyed the city of San Francisco, and he made a killing.

He again obtained huge profits from short positions before the crashes of 1907 and 1929. Despite of this, when he committed suicide in the Sherry Netherland Hotel in Manhattan in 1941, not much of it was left. How he came to lose his vast fortune was never definitely established, but probably several causes, including a complicated familiar life with three divorces, concurred to it.

The perennial bestseller *"Reminiscences of a Stock Operator"*, by writer and journalist Edwin Lefèvre, is, in fact, the financial biography of Livermore, starting with his betting times as bucket shops days and ending before the 1929 crash.

In 1940, prompted by his son Jesse Jr., Livermore published "*How to Trade in Stocks*," about his experiences and methods of trading. Unlike Lefèvre's book, it never caught on.

---

1. The so-called bucket shops were abundant in number and very popular at the time. They presented themselves as a stock exchange business, but in reality, were no more than shady betting establishments.

1

A market is the combined behavior of thousands of people responding to information, misinformation, and whim.

— KENNETH CHANG

			6	5		9		
	6		3	7	9			
9				1				
	9	3	8			1	4	
		2		6		5		
1		6	9			7		
6		9	7	8	3	2		
			1	4		9	6	
		4			6		3	7

212

2

I believe in analysis and not forecasting.

— NICOLAS DARVAS

					7		8	
	6	7						
1	8	3				7		
3	9	5	2	4		8		
			7	1				9
		8	3			6	2	4
	7				9	5		
8	3		5	2	4		6	
		4	6	7	1			3

213

3

Markets are constantly in a state of uncertainty and flux and money is made by discounting the obvious and betting on the unexpected.

— GEORGE SOROS

1		6		2	3		5	9
			5	9	7			8
	9				6		4	2
		8			2	9	3	
	4		3	5	9	8		
		9	7	1	8	2		
		5	9	7		4		6
9	7	1	8	6			2	3
8				5				7

214

4

The price of a commodity will never go to zero. When you invest in commodities futures, you're not buying a piece of paper that says you own an intangible piece of company that can go bankrupt.

— JIM ROGERS

3	6	1		8		9	4	
	8			4				3
	7	9	1			5	2	8
1	3		5	2	8		9	4
	2						6	1
9			6	1				
			4	7	9	1		
7		4	3			2		
6		3	8		2	4		

215

5

Buy not on optimism, but on arithmetic.

— BENJAMIN GRAHAM

6

This company looks cheap, that company looks cheap, but the overall economy could completely screw it up. The key is to wait. Sometimes the hardest thing to do is to do nothing.

— DAVID TEPPER

7						4	1	3
			1	3	4	2	6	7
4	1				2			
	5					7	2	6
3		1	2	6				
6	7			8		3		1
8	9		3				7	2
	3			2	6	9	5	8
	6			5	8			4

217

7

A broker named Tod moved to Texas and bought a donkey from an old farmer named Ben for $100. The farmer agreed to deliver the donkey the next day.
 The next day, Ben drove up to Tod's house with the donkey.
 Ben: Sorry, but I have some bad news. The donkey died.

Tod: Well, that's too bad. Give me the money back then.
 Ben: Can't do that. I went and spent it already.

Tod: OK, then. Unload the donkey, please.

Ben: It's dead! What are you going to do with him?

Tod: I'm going to raffle him off.

Ben: You can't raffle off a dead donkey!

Tod: I sure can. Watch me.

Some days later Ben drove up again to Tod's house.

Ben: So what happened with that dead donkey after all?

Tod: I raffled him off as I said I would. I sold 500-hundred tickets at five dollars apiece and made a profit of $2,495.

Ben: Didn't anyone complain?

Tod: Just the guy who won. I gave him his five dollars back, and that was that.

— UNKNOWN

			8	5	2		1	
							8	5
				1				
			7			9	1	
5			9	3	6		8	4
			6	1		8	2	5
1			7	8	5	2	6	9
8			2			3	6	7	1
9	3					7		

271

8

If you owe the bank $100 that's your problem. If you owe the bank $100 million, that's the bank's problem.

— JOHN PAUL GETTY

			8	1	4		5	
			6	9		2	5	1		8
					3			4
1	3		9					
	4	8			7		1	3
				1	3	8	9	
6	5	4	2	1		3		9
2	1	7			3	4		
		3	6					1

218

9

You can't listen to the news. You have to go with the facts. You need to use a logical approach and have the discipline to apply it. You must be able to control your emotions.

— BLAIR HULL

5		3			2	4		9
								1
		9						2
	8	7		9		3		
	4			3				7
3	5		2		7	9	4	
1		5	7		8	6	9	4
7			4		9		1	3
	9	4		1				

219

10

Money goes where money is.

— SPANISH PROVERB

		1					4	
7	6			4	9		3	1
4			3					6
	4		5		1	6		7
1			7	6	2			
	7						5	3
6				9	8			
			1	5	3	7	6	2
		1	5			6	9		4

220

11

Look down, not up, when making your initial investment decision. If you don't lose money, most of the remaining alternatives are good ones.

— JOEL GREENBLATT

	1	2			3		
2		9	3		7	8	
	6			7	4		
9	2	4	6				7
		6		1	9		
	8		2		6		
1		8	4		3	5	
				6	7		1
	3	5	1	8	4		2

221

12

I don't believe anything unless I understand it inside out. And even if I understand something, it is not uncommon that I disagree with accepted view (even if it's a Nobel laureate).

— MICHAEL BURRY

		2					1	7
		4				2	3	8
		1	2	3	8			5
		8	9					
4	9							3
1	7		8	2				9
		7	3		2	5		
8		3	4		5			
			1	7		3	8	2

222

13

Tom: Can I borrow that book of yours "How To Become A Millionaire"?
Tim: Sure, here you are.
Tom: Thanks, but why are half the pages missing?
Tim: Well, isn't half a million enough for you?

— UNKNOWN

JESSE LIVERMORE

6				4				1
	7			3			6	8
3	1	9	5	6				
9		8					2	3
	4	7	1		3			6
		1				5		
					9		8	5
1	9	6	4			3		2
		4			2	6	1	

223

14

What's worth doing is worth doing for money.

— GORDON GEKKO (WALL STREET)

	4	3		5	6			9
6	8	5						
		2			1			5
						9	2	7
	6		2	7	9			3
		9	1	4			6	8
2						8	5	
		3	5	6		7		
8	5	6			7	3	1	

224

15

Novice traders trade three to five times too big. They are taking 5 to 10 percent risks on a trade when they should be taking 1 to 2 percent risks. The emotional burden of trading is substantial. If you personalize these losses, you can't trade.

— BRUCE KOVNER

225

16

Don't gamble. Take all your savings and buy some good stock and hold it until it goes up, then sell it. If it don't go up, don't buy it.

— WILL ROGERS

			6		3	1	7	
9				7		9		8
	7	5	9	2	8		4	3
		7	5	9				4
	9			6	4			
8	6	4			7			2
			2			3		
	8	6						
4			7	5	9	2		6

226

17

Men are like bank accounts. Without a lot of money, they don't generate a lot of interest.

— UNKNOWN

8				4		3	1	6
9			6					
								2
		2			5		4	
			9		4	2		1
4	9			2	3		5	8
		3	9	1			7	4
				8	7	9		3
		8		9	2			

227

18

I am always prepared to do the right thing regardless of what other people think.

— BILL ACKMAN

	9				3		7	
3	2	1		5		8		
					4	1		2
	4	9		2	8	6	1	
8							5	4
1		6	4	9		2		
			5		6	3		8
6		4	8			7		
				7	2	4	6	

228

19

There's no such thing as a free lunch.

— MILTON FRIEDMAN

9	2			4			8	
				1	8		2	
			7	9				4
1	8	3	2			4	6	
7			6	5	4			
4			8		1			2
	7	9	4	6	5			
5		6			3	2		
3	1	8		2	7		4	

229

20

After the ship has sunk everyone knows how she might have been saved.

— ITALIAN PROVERB

3		9					2	
1		7	2	6	8	3		
8		6	3	5	9	7	1	4
7	1							
6	8	2		3	5		7	
9		5					8	2
4			1	8	2			
2							4	
		3		7			6	8

230

21

All men are frauds. The only difference between them is that some admit it. I myself deny it.

— H. L. MENCKEN

5		6		8				
2	8		4	3			6	
				1	6		2	
	4	3	6			8		2
6	5						7	
9		8	7	4	3		1	
1	6	5	9			4	3	7
				7			5	
3					5			9

231

22

Practical investors usually learn their problem is finding enough outstanding investments, rather than choosing among too many.

— PHILIP FISHER

5	2	3					9	1
				1			2	
					3	5	8	4
6					2	3	4	5	8
		2				4		7	1
4							3		2
	4		6		2		3	
2		9						7
	3		4	7	1			9

232

23

Fearless forecast, quoted in The Wall Street Journal: "Oil prices will go up or down, more or less, unless there are some unforeseen circumstances."

— UNKNOWN

9	6	5			1			
8		3		7	2		5	
			6	5		3		1
7	2	4		6	5			8
5	9		1	3	8	4		2
3		1	2	4				
			5	9		8	1	
	6	5	8			2	4	
		3		2				

233

24

It is better to have a permanent income than to be fascinating.

— OSCAR WILDE

5	6			4		1		
9			8				6	2
1	8			6		3		4
		8	2	5	6	4	3	
	5	6		9		7	1	
	9					2	5	6
		1		2	5	9		
				3	9	8		
4	3	9		1		6		5

234

25

If you don't own Gold, you know neither history nor economics.

— RAY DALIO

2						3		
			4	8	3			
	4				2	9		
		2		7	1			
			3	6		5		
8		6			5			7
6		9				7		2
	5			2			8	9
		2	8	9	6			

235

26

The stock market is designed to transfer money from the active to the patient.

— WARREN BUFFETT

	8		2	5	7		9	
			1			4		
1					6	7	2	
9	1	3	6					2
	6		7		5	1		9
7		5	9	1	3		4	6
	9					5		
	4	6	5		2			
5	7			9				4

236

27

Business is the art of extracting money from another man's pocket without resorting to violence.

— MAX AMSTERDAM

						7	9	4
	8		7	9		2	5	3
	4	7			3			8
2	1	8	4	6	9	3		
6	9	4	3	7			2	
		5		8		4		
3	2		9		6			7
8		9		4		1		
		5	1	3			8	

237

28

I never hesitate to tell a man that I am bullish or bearish. But I do not tell people to buy or sell any particular stock. In a bear market all stocks go down and in a bull market they go up.

— JESSE LIVERMORE

	4	5			8		9		7
						9			
			7		2	4	8		6
				9			5		
7							6	8	
2	4			3	6			9	
				8	3	6	1	7	9
	3		8	7	9		4		
							3	6	8

238

29

If all you have is a hammer in the toolbox, everything looks like a nail.

— BERNARD BARUCH

	3		2	9				
9		2	7					3
1	7	4		8	5	9	6	2
2	9	6	1	7		3		
	1	7	5	3	8			
	5	3		2	9		1	
		9				5		
7	4	1						9
		8			2			1

239

30

Getting money is like digging with a needle. Spending it is like water soaking into the sand.

— JAPANESE PROVERB

	2	8				7	4	
		5	7	4	9		8	6
4		7	2		6			3
		2			1		7	4
		5	9	7				8
7						3	1	
	6	2	1		3	4	9	
			4		7		6	
			8		2	5		1

240

31

Bitcoin will do to banks what email did to the postal industry.

— RICK FALKVINGE

		5	1	6				7
	6		7	9				
9	2		5	3	1			8
	1		2	7		5		
			4			1		
5						7		2
	1			2				5
2	7		5		6		1	
4	5	3	1			2		9

241

CHARLES (CHARLIE) MUNGER

Born on January 1st in 1924, in Nebraska, Charlie Munger's first job was as a cashier at the grocery store Buffet & Son where he worked. His boss was Warren Buffett's grandfather.

Set on studying mathematics, he enrolled at the University of Michigan but left in 1943 to join the US Army Air Corps, where he learned the valuable skill of card playing, which taught him when to fold and when to bet strongly.

He earned his J.D. magna cum laude from Harvard Law School without ever receiving an undergraduate degree.

Relocating to California, he founded the prestigious law firm of Munger, Tolles & Olson LLP dedicating himself to real estate law, later becoming a real estate developer and running an investment partnership. He was chair of Wesco Financial Corporation, the

Daily Journal Corporation, and a director of Costco Wholesale Corporation.

A true polymath, Munger has also studied meteorology and architecture and designed his own house.

This long-term friend and partner of Warren Buffett is today worth close to 1.8 billion dollars. He his a significant benefactor of both his alma mater and Stanford University, and made considerable donations to other educational institutions such as the Kavli Institute for Theoretical. He chose not to sign *The Giving Pledge*[1] endorsed by his friends Warren Buffet and Bill Gates.

The celebrated *"Poor Charlie's Almanack"* conveys his *"elementary, worldly wisdom"* philosophy as it relates to the world of finance and business and contains many *mungerisms*, as his quotations and pithy comments are known.

---

1. A campaign that encourages wealthy people to contribute a substantial part of their wealth to philanthropy.

1

From a trader after a market crash: "This is worse than a divorce. I've lost half my net worth and I still have a wife."

— UNKNOWN

			5		9	2	6		3	4
								5		1
			8		7		5			
3	1	5	6		2			8		
7						4		5		
9				5		1	2			7
		1	2		5			9		6
5	7		4			9				8
6	9	4			8	3				

242

2

There are old traders; and there are bold traders; but there are no old bold traders.

— WALL STREET SAYING

	1	3				9	7		2
		8				6		4	1
		7	6	1	3			9	5
	4			9	2		1		
		2		6	1	3		8	4
		1			5	8	2		9
	8			7		1		5	3
		6	1		4	5			
		4						1	

243

3

Indigents are poor. Hate the poor. Can't pay.

— DENNY CRANE (WILLIAM SHATNER), BOSTON LEGAL

		6	8					
				3	2			6
7		2		6	1			
		5		8		3	2	7
9		4	2	7	3		1	
								4
5								
	9	8		2	7	5		
	2	7	6		5	4		8

244

4

There's danger in just shoveling out money to people who say, 'My life is a little harder than it used to be.' At a certain place you've got to say to the people, 'Suck it in and cope, buddy. Suck it in and cope.

— CHARLIE MUNGER

			6		5	1			2	
			3			8			6	9
			4		2		5	6		
						7			2	4
				3					5	6
			2					5	3	
			9	5		3			2	4
			7	1	3			8	9	
			8				6		7	1

245

5

Amateurs go broke taking large losses, professionals go broke taking small profits.

— WILLIAM ECKHARDT

		7			5		2	
	5	8		3				
		2	9		7			
9						6	7	2
8		4		2		1	5	9
		7	5		1	3	4	8
4	2	6				3		
7		1	3		8		6	4
	8		6		2	9		

246

6

My problem lies in reconciling my gross habits with my net income.

— ERROL FLYNN

1	8		6	3		7		
		9	7				5	1
	7				5	6		
9		3	2		4			
4	2					8		6
	1				3	2		
7	4	2		5				
8		1				4	2	7
		6	4			5	1	

247

7

Investors often make the mistake of equating manager performance in a given year with manager skill. In fact, during market bubbles, the best performers are often the most imprudent rather than the most skilled managers.

— JACK SCHWAGER

						4	6	
	3	2			4	5		7
	4					8		2
2	9		1					3
6		1	3			2		4
		3	4	2				
				3		4	6	5
	2	9	5	4		1	7	8
4	6	5	8		7		2	

248

8

The quant's girlfriend: "Do you love your math more than me?"
"Of course not, dear - I love you much more."
"Then prove it!"
"OK... Let R be the set of all lovable objects..."

— UNKNOWN

	6	1			9			
		9		5	2	1		
8	5	2	4		1			
1				9		6		
					6	3		7
		6					9	
6		7		9		4		2
			5	2	4		6	
	2	4		1	7	8	3	

249

9

If the rich could hire other people to die for them, the poor could make a wonderful living.

— JEWISH PROVERB

		2				4	5	
	6			4		3		
4			2		8		6	
		8			1	7		
2	1		5	7	4		3	8
					3		1	
8			4	6	7	5	9	3
6	7		3				2	
		3	1	8		6	7	4

250

10

After a while size means nothing. It gets back to whether you're making 100% rate of return on $10,000 or $100 million dollars. It doesn't make any difference.

— PAUL TUDOR JONES

				6				
5			9	2	7	3	4	
9						6	8	
4			8	5	6			2
8	5	6			2	1	3	4
7					4	5	6	
	8		2	7		4	1	3
		9				8	5	6
3	4	1	6			2	7	9

251

11

Sign on a gas station: "We collect taxes — federal, state, and local. We also sell gasoline as a sideline."

— UNKNOWN

3	9		1				8	
		2	8	5	4	7		
		5	3	9	7	2		6
2	8	5	4			6		1
			1	6	5	2		
7					5	9		3
	2			4		1	9	
	4	3		7		6		
	7	1		2		5		

252

12

Try to figure out what your skill set is and apply that to the markets. If you are really good at accounting, you might be good as a value investor. If you are strong in computers and math, you might do best with a quantitative approach.

— EDWARD THORP

		9				5	2	
	1						7	8
	5		9	7	8			1
4	6			5			9	7
2				9	7		4	
	7	8	6					
1	4		2					
	2	3		8	9		1	
8		7	4	6	1		3	

253

13

What do you call a stock that's down 90%? A stock that was down 80% and then got cut in half.

— DAVID EINHORN

3				2		4		1
8		2		4	9	3	6	7
		9	3			5	2	8
				1		7		
	1		7					
	3				2			9
	9							
6	7	3		8		9		4
	2	8	4	9	1	6		3

254

14

A gold-mine is just a hole in the ground with a liar at the top.

— MARK TWAIN

3	7	8	2				9	4
5	1	2			6	7		
4				3			2	5
2		6	7		3	5		
		7			5			
	5	1		2		3		
		3	5			2	4	1
7		5	4	1	2		3	
1					9			

256

15

My philosophy is that all stocks are bad. There are no good stocks unless they go up in price. If they go down instead, you have to cut your losses fast Letting losses run is the most serious mistake made by most investors.

— WILLIAM O'NEIL

						5		
3	1		9	8	5	2	4	
	5		4		2	1		
4			2		3			
	3			9	8			
9				4	6		2	
5	4		6	2	7	9		1
		6		1	9	4		5
			8	5	4	7	6	2

257

16

The relationship between knowledge and money can be explained by a few mathematical equations:

Postulate 1: Knowledge = Power
Postulate 2: Time = Money
And as:
- Power = Work / Time

Substituting we have:
- Knowledge = Work / Money

Solving for money, we get:
- Money = Work / Knowledge.

Thus, as knowledge approaches zero, money approaches infinity, and this is independent of the amount of work.

Corollary: The less you know, the more money you make.

— UNKNOWN

			4	6	3	9	5	
3	4	6	5	2	9			1
	5		7	1		3		6
2						6	9	
1		4		5		2		
6					2	1		4
			6	9		5	2	8
						7	1	
	2				7	4	6	

285

17

Speculators often prosper through ignorance; it is a cliché that in a roaring bull market knowledge is superfluous and experience is a handicap. But the typical experience of the speculator is one of temporary profit and ultimate loss.

— BENJAMIN GRAHAM

	2	1	5	3			
4	5				6	7	
						5	
6	9			7	2	5	3	4
	7	2			3	8	6	9
			6			7		1
	3		8					
		9		1				3
2		7	3	4		8		

258

18

If you're going to panic, panic early.

— UNKNOWN

	9	2					3	4	6
1	8		3	4	6		2	7
	3				7			1
	1		6			7	9	4
5	6	3	7			1	8	
				8		6		
9		1	5					
			6		7	3	2	
			7		1			8

259

19

Flies will easily fly into the honey — their problem is how to get out.

— PERSIAN PROVERB

	3			4	5		9	8
		5		9				1
	9	8				4		
	6	4	8	7	9	1		2
8	7	9	1					5
			5	6		8		
9		7	2	1		5		
3			4	5	6	9		7
4		6		8				

260

20

I just want to be rich enough to be referred to as eccentric instead of just nuts.

— UNKNOWN

		3		4	5		9	8
		5		9				1
	9	8				4		
	6	4	8	7	9	1		2
8	7	9	1					5
			5	6		8		
9		7	2	1		5		
3				4	5	6	9	7
4		6		8				

261

21

Rule #1: Never lose money.

Rule #2: Never forget rule #1.

— WARREN BUFFETT

			7	3				
5	7	3	8	6		4	9	
				9		5		
		4	5	7				
3	5		1		6	2		
8			2		9	3		
			3		7		6	1
7				1	8	9	2	
1			9	2	4	7	3	

262

22

Probability is not a mere computation of odds on the dice or more complicated variants; it is the acceptance of the lack of certainty in our knowledge and the development of methods for dealing with our ignorance.

— NASSIM TALEB

			2	9			1	8
9	4		1	8				
			3	5	6	2	9	4
		5			9			
	9			1	8			
1			6	3			2	
	6		9	4		1	8	7
4	2	9			1	3	5	
					3	9	4	2

263

23

They say money can't buy happiness. Look at the fucking smile on my face. Ear to ear, baby.

— JIM YOUNG (BOILER ROOM)

6	8		1		9	7	2	5
						6		
	2				8			1
5		2			7	1		
	7			1	6	5		2
	6		2			3		
		4						
	5					2		
	3	6			1	8	5	

264

24

The borrowers will always be willing to take a great deal for themselves. It's up to the lenders to show restraint, and when they lose it, watch out.

— MICHAEL BURRY

			2					9
3	7							6
		8	6					3
		7			6	5		
		1	5				7	
4	3				8	9	1	
			3		8	2		
7	8	3			2		6	5
1	2	9	6	5			3	7

265

25

You learn in this business: If you want a friend, get a dog.

— CARL ICAHN

2	9	6				8	4	
				7	4			2
7	4	3	9		2	8		1
	2	9		5				
1	8	5	4	3				6
		4			6		8	
	3					5		
	6	2	1		5		7	
	1		7				2	9

266

26

If you want to make a lot of money, resist diversification.

— JIM ROGERS

	4							
			3			9	4	1
3			9	4		5	6	
	5			3			9	
		4						7
8		6	2	5	7	1	3	
6	1							3
			4	2	3		1	9
		3	6	1	9	7		

267

27

Calling someone who trades actively an investor is like calling someone who repeatedly engages in one-night stands a romantic.

— WARREN BUFFET

		2						
8	4		7	6			2	
			2	5	3	8		1
1		4		7	6	5		
		7	3	2				
	3	2	4	1	8			
2	5		8	4				
		8		9	7			5
7		9			2		1	8

268

28

At the stock market you have to behave as if you take a bath in cold waters: jump in and get out again quickly.

— CARL MEYER ROTHSCHILD

		2	7		9	3		
	6	9	8			2	1	
		3		5		6		
				7	6		3	4
	7		4		3		2	1
3				1			6	9
		2	6		7			
		9	3	4				
8	3		5	2				6

269

29

In this business if you're good, you're right six times out of ten. You're never going to be right nine times out of ten.

— PETER LYNCH

	8	2		7	6		1	
	4		1				2	3
	9	1	8	2		6		
2			6	4			9	1
		4			5		8	2
1	5	9	3	8	2		6	
		1	5		3		4	7
8	2		7		4		5	9
					1	2	3	

272

30

Successful investing is anticipating the anticipations of others.

— JOHN MAYNARD KEYNES

2			1	5			3	
8	5		4				2	6
			9	2	6	1	8	5
1								2
4	7		3				1	
	2	3				5	4	
			7	3	9		6	
		7		6				4
	1	2	8		4		3	9

273

JAMES (JIM) ROGERS

Born in Maryland in 1942 and raised in Alabama, Rogers attended Yale University, where he graduated in History. Two years later he got a second degree from the University of Oxford, a BA in Politics, Economics and Philosophy.

In 1970, at investment bank *Arnhold and S. Bleichroderher*, he met and worked with George Soros. Three years later they left the bank and founded the Quantum Fund, one of the first international funds.

The extraordinary returns of the fund made Rogers a millionaire. In 1980 he decided to retire and travel around the world on a motorbike.

He made over 100,000 miles with his motorcycle, a feat that got him in the Guinness Book of World Records. He got his second Guinness World Record for traveling over 245,000 kilometers across 116 countries in a custom-made Mercedes, in the company of his wife, Paige.

He recounted his experiences in "Investment Biker: Around the World with Jim Rogers" and "Adventure Capitalist: The Ultimate Road Trip," who both become bestsellers. A prolific author, he also penned "Hot Commodities: How Anyone Can Invest Profitably in the World's Best Market", "Street Smarts: Adventures on the Road and in the Markets", "A Bull in China: Investing Profitably in the World's Greatest Market", and "A Gift to My Children: A Father's Lessons for Life and Investing".

Rogers founded the Rogers International Commodity Index, was a guest professor at Columbia Business School and a frequent guest on several financial television shows.

In 2007 Rogers moved with his family to Singapore famously saying that if you were smart in the 19th century, you moved to London, if you were smart in the 20th century, you moved to New York, and if you are smart in the 21st century, you move to Asia.

1

It's not whether you're right or wrong that's important, but how much money you make when you're right and how much you lose when you're wrong.

— GEORGE SOROS

3	2			9		8		
	9		6			2		3
6	8				7	9		
7		9		6	8			
	6	8	1					
1	3					6	8	5
		6		1				
		3					6	
		7		5	6			

274

2

Never risk more than 1% of your total equity in any one trade. By risking 1%, I am indifferent to any individual trade. Keeping your risk small and constant is absolutely critical.

— LARRY HITE

		8		5	7	3		2
9			1	2			6	4
		3	6		8	7		
			8	9	5			
				1		4		6
	1		3	6		5	8	
	8	9	5			6		
	7	1	2	3	6			8
		6						

275

3

Acquaintance: a person whom we know well enough to borrow from, but not well enough to lend to.

— AMBROSE BIERCE

		6	9		2		3	
8	2			5	1		7	
					7			9
6	7	4		9		5		3
9	8	2						
	1	3	7			6	9	2
4			7		2	9		1
2						3		
3						2		8

276

4

The four most dangerous words in investing are: "This time it's different".

— JOHN TEMPLETON

9			5					
8	2	5			4			3
	1			6	9		2	5
5			4	1	7	3		
	4		9				8	
		3		5	8	7		
2	5	8			1	9		6
1					3		5	8
	6	9	8		5	1	7	

277

5

Never bend the rules. You bend the rules a little bit and then it's a slippery slope.

— THOMAS PETERFFY

				1	8	6	7	
8		1			3			
5					2		8	6
						8	3	7
1					5			
	5	3			2	1		6
		8	5	3				4
		5	2		4		1	8
2		4	8				3	7

278

6

The market is never wrong. Traders are wrong.

— JESSE LIVERMORE

9		8		2	6		1	4
6		2	3		4		8	
		3	7	8	9		2	
1	9			5	8	4		
	6					9		
2	4	3				6		
	8	6	2	4			9	
5				1				7
3				6	7	2		

279

7

Debts are like children: the smaller they are the more noise they make.

— SPANISH PROVERB

5		7	1					
			9					
	9			7		6	1	3
	3	6	4	9		5		
2	4		5	8		3		
7	5		6	1		4	9	
					1	2	4	9
					9	8		5
	2			5	8	1		

280

8

Why is that so important to everyone, maintaining integrity?

— ALAN SHORE (JAMES SPADER), BOSTON LEGAL

1	2		9	4	6		8	
9	4		3		8		5	
3				2		4		9
	1				2	4		
	9			3	4	1		
	3	4		1		9		6
2		1		8	9		3	
	8			5				
7		3						

281

9

Believe me, there's nothing better than buying from someone who has to sell regardless of price during a crash. Many of the best buys we've ever made occurred for that reason.

— HOWARD MARKS

10

It's time, not timing, that makes money in the market.

— UNKNOWN

1	2	8	6			7	3	
5	6	4	3	9		2	8	1
					1			4
					4	9	7	
	5	6		3				
	9		1	2	8	4		
		1	4	5	6		9	7
6		5	9			8		
		9		1	2	6		

283

11

When buying and selling are controlled by legislation, the first things to be bought and sold are legislators.

— P. J. O'ROURKE

			8	7		4	6	1
				6	4	9		
			6		9		7	3
	1		4	8	2			
	2	4	9	7		1	5	6
7					1			
5		3	1	4	8			
		1	2	9	7			5
		7	3	5	6	8	1	4

284

12

There's many a pessimist who got that way by financing an optimist.

— UNKNOWN

4	6					8		
9		5	8			6	1	
		3	6	1	4		5	
				8		4		1
3		7		6	1	9	2	
1		6		9				7
6		4						8
		9	7	3	8		4	
	3	8					9	2

286

13

If you do not keep your shares when their price falls, you will not own them when their price rises.

— ANDRÉ KOSTOLANY

			2	7				
			3	5	6			2
				9	2	7	4	3
1	5				9		4	
	9						3	1
4	8	2			5	3	6	7	9
2		9	3			5		
				7			2	4
			5		4	9		3

287

14

Making a speech on economics is a lot like pissing down your leg. It seems hot to you, but it never does to anyone else.

— LYNDON B. JOHNSON

			1		6			
7		1		3	4			2
	4	9	8	2	5			
				1	7		4	9
1	7	6		9	3		5	
					8	6	1	
6							2	5
4				5	8			1
2	5		7	6	1			

288

15

First, check whether the market as a whole is rising or falling. In other words, are you in a bull market or bear market? If the latter, stay out. The odds are against you.

— NICOLAS DARVAS

	3	1				9	7	6
			7	6	4			1
	7			1				
	4	7		3				2
		3	9				4	
		2	4			5	8	
	1	9		5	4	2		8
			2	6				
2	6	8	7			3		

289

16

*T*he poor's man toast always falls to the floor with the buttered side facing down.

— PORTUGUESE PROVERB

9	2		8		7			3
1				5	6	2		9
6	3	5						
8			6		5	9		4
							8	
	9		7			3		
3			4		2		7	8
	4		1		8	6		5
7		1				4		2

290

17

If you ever find yourself tempted to seek out someone else's opinion on a trade, that's usually a sure sign that you should get out of your position.

— LINDA BRADFORD RASCHKE

		2	9			7	1	
			4		1	3	5	
	4	7	2			6	8	
7	1			4	3			8
3			8	2		9		
			1	9	7		3	
	3	1	6		2			7
2		5			9			
9		8	3			5		6

291

18

The more you think you know, the more closed-minded you'll be.

— RAY DALIO

	2			3		6	7	8
		1		7	8		2	4
	7	8				9	3	
	9	3		6	7	8	5	
1		7			2		9	3
8		2	4	9			6	
	8			4	9		1	
	4				6	7		5
			7	8			4	9

292

19

The haves and have-nots can often be traced back to the *dids* and *did-nots*.

— UNKNOWN

1	5	7			2	6	4	9
	2		4			5		
	6	4			5		8	3
	9	6		4		3		7
	1						6	8
					9	1	5	
						7		5
6				5		8		2
	7	3	9		8		1	6

293

20

I try to buy stock in businesses that are so wonderful that an idiot can run them. Because sooner or later, one will.

— WARREN BUFFETT

			5	2	1			3
				8		7		9
	3	4		6		5	2	1
4	2	3		7	8			6
7								
		1	3	4	2			8
	4	8		1		2	3	5
	7	6			5		9	4
3	5					6	1	7

294

21

I won $3 million on the lottery this weekend so I decided to donate a quarter of it to charity. Now I have $2,999,999.75.

— UNKNOWN

	6	4	1		9		2	7
1		9				3	6	4
		2	3	6		1	8	
4			9		2		3	6
9	5		7					
				1	8		5	2
		3				9		
6	4	1	8			2		
8	9		2			6		1

295

22

Someday I want to be rich. Some people get so rich they lose all respect for humanity. That's how rich I want to be.

— RITA RUDNER

	2	3			7		4	8
			8		4	2		1
4	8					6		
				9	6		5	
	6	7		8	5	1		3
5	4		1					6
		4	3		2	6		9
2	3	1		7			8	
7	9		5		8	3	1	

296

23

If you can afford to go first class and you don't, your heirs will.

— UNKNOWN

	9				3		7	1
3		8	4		1	2		
	7	1			2			
			1	4	7			
		7	2	5	9	8		6
			3	6	8		4	
9		5			6	7		
	8		7		4		9	
7	1		9	2		6	8	

297

24

Beggars do not envy millionaires, though of course they will envy other beggars who are more successful.

— BERTRAND RUSSELL

1	5		7	9				3
		6			8	5	2	1
3		8						7
				1		7	9	
8			2	7	9	3		
2	7				4			
5	2				3	1		
		6	4	8			7	5
		8	5	2				

298

25

In life you have to do a lot of things you don't fucking want to do. Many times, that's what the fuck life is... one vile fucking task after another.

— AL SWEARENGEN, (IAN MCSHANE), DEADWOOD

			9		
7	9	3	1	8		5
3	1			7		
7		3	1	2				
1			8		4	3		9
8		4	7	9	3	5		2
		6	4			3		
		9		1	2			
	1	2	5			9	4	7

299

26

With money you are a dragon, with no money, a worm.

— CHINESE PROVERB

		4	8	7	5	6		2
5		7	2	6				
		6			3	7		
7	9		3		6	8		
	3	1	5	8				9
				2	7	1	6	
2		3	4	5	1	9		
						3	2	
	7	9			2	5		4

300

27

TODAY IN THE STOCK MARKET:

- Helium was up; feathers were down.
- Paper was stationary.
- Fluorescent tubing was dimmed in light trading.
- Knives were up sharply.
- Cow steered into a bull market.
- Pencils lost a few points.
- Hiking equipment was trailing.

- Elevators rose, while escalators continued their slow decline.
- Weights were up in heavy trading.
- Light switches were off.
- Mining equipment hit rock bottom.
- Diapers remain unchanged.
- Shipping lines stayed on an even keel.
- The market for raisins dried up.
- Coca-Cola fizzled.
- Caterpillar stock inched up a bit.
- Sun peaked at midday
- Balloon prices were inflated.

— UNKNOWN

JAMES (JIM) ROGERS

3		6	9	2		4	8	
9		1			8	5	6	
7						2		
							2	1
6	7	5		3		9		8
		2	8	9	4	7	5	6
4						6	3	2
5				6			9	
2		3	4		9	8		

331

28

If you've got a dollar and you spend 29 cents on a loaf of bread, you've got 71 cents left; But if you've got seventeen grand and you spend 29 cents on a loaf of bread, you've still got seventeen grand. There's a math lesson for you.

— STEVE MARTIN

	7	3		5	1	4		9
5	1	6	2	9	4	3		
4	2						1	6
9		2	8		3		5	
3			1		5	9		2
	5		4				3	8
2				8				
7	3	8	5	1				
	6	5		4	2			

301

29

What's wealth but the means of expanding one's life? There's two ways one can do it: either by producing more or by producing it faster.

— AYN RAND

3	5		6	7		8		
	1	6	8	4		9		
		8					7	1
		1		9		5		7
9	3					1		
			1		4			
					9		5	6
	9	4			6	7	1	
			7	1		2		

302

30

There's always free cheese in a mousetrap.

— UNKNOWN

3				6		1		4
				4		7	3	
	7	3					5	9
8	4		2		3			5
	3			9		4		8
6					8	2	7	
1	8	4	3	2			9	
	7	3		5				
	6				1	3		7

303

31

I constantly see people rise in life who are not the smartest, sometimes not even the most diligent, but they are learning machines. They go to bed every night a little wiser than they were when they got up and boy does that help!

— CHARLIE MUNGER

			3		7	1		
8	7	3	1		6	9	2	4
5								7
1	5	7			2	4	3	8
9	2		4		8		1	5
				1	5			
		8	5					3
	9	5						
		3		7	1			9

304

GEORGE SOROS

Born György Schwartz in 1930 in Budapest, in what he described as an antisemitic Jewish home, he left Soviet-occupied Hungary to England in 1947. In 1936, to hide its Jewish roots, the family had changed their name to Soros.

In London, working part-time as a railway porter and as a nightclub waiter to make ends meet, Soros attended the London School of Economics. There he earned a Bachelor of Science in philosophy in 1951, and a Master of Science in philosophy in 1954. One of his teachers and mentors was the philosopher Karl Popper.

His career in finance started in the bank Singer & Friedlander in London. He worked his way from Clerck to the arbitrage department.

Moving to New York in 1956, he entered the world of finance and investments, where he was to make his fortune.

Inspired by the ideas of his mentor Karl Popper, Soros developed a market behavior theory he called reflexivity. It states that market participants' views and events influence each other in reflexive feedback loops leading to "virtuous" or "vicious" cycles of boom and bust.

In 1970, he launched his hedge fund, Soros Fund Management. From that year until 2011, when he closed the fund to outsiders and returned the money to his investors, he averaged over 20% per year compound returns, a fantastic performance.

Soros is known as "The Man Who Broke the Bank of England," an allusion to the old popular song performed by Charles Coborn, "The Man Who Broke the Bank at Monte Carlo." He earned that distinction on September 16, 1992, which became to be known as Black Wednesday. Soros's fund had a humungous short position on the sterling pound, which he considered grossly overvalued. When the UK government finally caved in and devaluated the pound, Soros netted an estimated 1 billion dollars of profit.

Through his Open Society Foundation Soros has made large philanthropic donations. He is also a significant contributor to liberal and progressive causes, some somewhat controversial, stating that he considers that doing so is his duty since he has the means and enjoys the independence others do not.

1

To attempt to increase the wealth of any country, by detaining in it an unnecessary quantity of gold, is as absurd as it would be to attempt to increase the good cheer of private families by obliging them to keep an unnecessary number of kitchen utensils.

— ADAM SMITH

	8	2		1	7	6	9	
		1	3	6	9	8	2	5
		9			2	1		4
			1	5	6		8	
2				7				9
			8	9	3	1		
6	2				7		4	1
8	7	5	1					
1				6		7	5	

305

2

Income, that is the thing. I wish an income that will keep flowing into my purse whether I sit on the wall or travel to far lands.

— GEORGE CLASON

	3			7	5			9
7		8	4		9	2		1
4		9	1			8	7	
1			5	8				
							2	
9						5	8	
6	9		2			7		
	1	2			8	6	9	
5	8	7	6	9				

306

3

Teacher: Would you trade you friends for money?
Student: Yes.
Teacher: Why?
Student: People change money doesn't.

— UNKNOWN

			9	7	3			
	7	3		8		2	5	6
	8					9		3
3							2	5
		8	2	5			9	
6	2		3	9		8		
	3	9	8	1	4			
8	1				5	7		
5			7		9	4		

307

4

Some people get rich studying artificial intelligence. Me, I make money studying natural stupidity.

— CARL ICAHN

		4	8		5	1		
	8							9
		2	3	9		5		
	3	9	5		7	2		
7	5			1				3
2	1	6		3	9		5	
6			9	4	3			
		3	7	5	8			1
8					1		9	4

308

5

Never try to walk across a river just because it has an average depth of four feet.

— MILTON FRIEDMAN

			4	7	1			9
				6	5	2		
9			5	8	4	2		7
1			3	5	9	6		
					4	3		7
		2				9		5
6		9			8	7		
8	4				7		9	
3						2	8	4

309

6

When a rich man falls, they say it was an accident; when a poor man falls they say that he was drunk.

— TURKISH PROVERB

		8					5	
						8		7
5	1		9	7				
	2					7		
				9	7			2
		7	3	6		5		
3	6	2		1			7	
			5	7		9	2	
			9	2	3		4	5

310

7

A good trend following system will keep you in the market until there is evidence that the trend has changed.

— RICHARD DENNIS

			7	9	4	2		
7					8	1		
		8		1	5			9
8					1	9	4	
1			4	7			2	
		9				3	1	5
	1	5	9		7		6	
	4		2	8				
	8	6			3	7	9	4

311

8

Anyone who lives within their means suffers from a lack of imagination.

— OSCAR WILDE

	8	2					6	4
7	9	5		4	1	3	8	2
	6	4					9	5
		6		8				9
				9			3	6
	1	9	3		2	5	7	8
9		7		1	6			
	2	1				9		7
				7	9	6		1

312

9

The trend is your friend.

— WALL STREET SAYING

		8		6	9	5	2		1
9	5	6		1		7		8	4
2				1	4		8		
		9	8				2	4	3
		2	5	7		3			
		3		8	6	9			5
8				9					
				2	7				
7	4					6	5		9

313

10

The desire to maximize the number of winning trades (or minimize the number of losing trades) works against the trader. The success rate of trades is the least important performance statistic and may even be inversely related to performance.

— WILLIAM ECKHARDT

314

11

It can require patience and fortitude to hold positions long enough to be proved right.

— HOWARD MARKS

12

If you can't take a small loss, sooner or later you will take the mother of all losses.

— ED SEYKOTA

		7				9		
	1	9		6	4		2	7
		4	2	7				
4	3		5	2				8
	2	6		8	7			3
9				3		6		
6		3	7			8	1	4
	9	2			8		6	
	4	8	6		3			

316

13

In a bear market, you have to use sharp countertrend rallies to sell.

— BRUCE KOVNER

			2			3	6	
			3	6	5	1	4	7
5		6		4	7			
4	7	3	9				2	
				2		7	3	
	5				4	9		
	4				1	6		2
				9		4		3
2	6		4	5			7	1

317

14

I also learned the value of withholding judgement until I could make a decision based on evidence.

— EDWARD THORP

7		6	2		8	1	3	
	8			3	4	6	7	
	4		6	7	5			8
2	9	5	8	1		4		
1	3					5		
6			5	2	9	8		3
		7				3	4	6
				4	6			
	6	3	7	5	2			

318

15

Mentor, n.: someone whose hindsight can become your foresight.

— UNKNOWN

	4	6	7	3	1	9		
			2		9	5	4	
9		8	5				7	3
			9		8			4
8			6	5			1	
	5	4					9	
4	6	5		1	7			9
3	1		8		2			5
2		9	4		5	7		

319

16

Spend words as efficiently as money.

— JAPANESE PROVERB

						2	1	
	8		7	2			3	4
	1	7				5	8	
7	9	3	8			6		1
4		8		6	2	7		
6		1	3	7		4		
			9		7			5
1	7	9	5	3	4		6	
	4	5	2			1		

320

17

The biggest mistake investors make is to believe that what happened in the recent past is likely to persist. Typically, high past returns simply imply that an asset has become more expensive and is a poorer, not better, investment.

— RAY DALIO

321

18

Wall Street is the only place that people ride to in a Rolls Royce to get advice from those who take the subway.

— WARREN BUFFETT

			6	1			5	8		4
2	3	5	4					1	9	
	8	7	9	6	1	3	5			
7	4					2	6	5		
			5					7		
5			7	4	3		8	1		
	1		6	5				3		
	5		3					8		
3				1						

322

19

*I*f investing is entertaining, if you're having fun, you're probably not making any money. Good investing is boring.

— GEORGE SOROS

		8			9	7	2		4
9	7					2	6	8	5
				5					9
					4	2			1
	2			1		8		7	
			8	7			4	2	6
6	4				1		3		7
			5			3			
7	3	9		6		1			

323

20

Risk no more that you can afford to lose, but risk enough so that a win is meaningful.

— ED SEYKOTA

324

21

I always believe that prices move first, and fundamentals come second.

— PAUL TUDOR JONES

				3	6		5	9
	6		5	9			1	
9	2		1	7	8	6		
				5	9	7		1
5			2	1				
		2	8		3		6	
2				8		3		
8			3	6	5			
	5			2	1	4		

325

22

I've seen a lot more stocks go to zero than infinity.

— JAMES CHANOS

				3	6		5	9
	6		5	9			1	
9	2		1	7	8	6		
				5	9	7		1
5			2	1				
		2	8		3		6	
2				8			3	
8			3	6	5			
	5			2	1	4		

326

23

Zimbabwe's stock market was the best performer this decade — but your entire portfolio now buys you 3 eggs.

— KYLE BASS

4	3					1	5	
	8			5	6		4	3
5	6		3		4	8	7	
1	5			3		2	8	
	4			8	7	6	1	5
7					5	3		4
				4				
	9	4	7		8	5	6	1
8		2	5			4		9

327

24

Early on, people invested in me because of my letters and then, somehow, after they invested, they stopped reading them.

— MICHAEL BURRY

7		9						1
		2		1		3		7
					7	4		2
	1	5		3		2		6
	7	3		6				
		4	5	8	1		3	9
5					3		2	
3	9		2	4	6			
6	2		1	5	8	9	7	

328

25

I have noticed that everyone who has ever tried to tell me that markets are efficient is poor.

— LARRY HITE

	4	1			7	6		
	8	7	5	6	9	1	3	
		5		3				
1	3		7	2	8			
		8	9				1	
5		9		1				
		2	6	9			4	1
9			3	4	1			
4	1	3	8	7			5	

329

26

The art is not in making money, but in keeping it.

— DUTCH PROVERB

		5		8				
	2							1
	7	9			4			
	6	7			5		8	4
	3	1	4					6
8	4		6	7	9		5	
7	8	6		3			2	5
1	9	3						8
							1	9

330

27

The only thing I do know is that from chaos comes opportunity.

— DANIEL S. LOEB

```
2 6 5 |   1 8 | 3
      | 9 3   | 5 2
      | 6   2 |   8 4
------+-------+------
    6 | 7 4   | 5
3 7 4 | 2 9   | 1
5 2   |     1 |
------+-------+------
  3 8 | 5 7   |
  5   | 1     |   4 3
6 1 2 |       | 7
```

332

28

There is no point in being confident and having a small position.

— GEORGE SOROS

		9	4	8	3	6	5	7
			6		7	1		9
6		7	9	1	2			3
9	1	2	3	4			6	
4	8	3	7	6		9		
7	6	5			1			
								1
		6		2	9			4
			8		4	5	7	

29

Short-term market and economic prognostication is largely a fool's errand, we invest according to a strategy that makes the need to rely on short-term market or economic assessments largely irrelevant.

— BILL ACKMAN

7	4			5				
					6	3		4
				4	3		1	5
3	9		2	7	5	8		
		5		1			3	
	1	8	3		4	5		7
	2		4			5		
4	6		5	3	7			2
			8			4		

334

30

The young man knows the rules, but the old man knows the exceptions.

— OLIVER WENDELL HOLMES

			3	8		4			5
		4		7	2	5	1		3
5	7				3	1			
8	9			5				1	
2				1	6				
				4	8	9	5		2
					1		8		4
				9		8	2		
4	8	9		2	5	7	6	3	1

335

EDUARD (ED) THORP

Ed Thorp is a polymath hedge-fund manager, mathematics professor, investor, blackjack player, and author.

Born in Chicago in 1932, he received his Ph.D. in mathematics from the University of California in 1958 and taught at the Massachusetts Institute of Technology (MIT) from 1959 to 1961. He subsequently taught mathematics and finance at New Mexico State University and the University of California at Irvine.

He used an IBM mainframe computer as a research tool to improve the odds of winning at blackjack. His game theory was successfully tested in practice using $10,000 provided by Manny Kimmel, a wealthy professional gambler and one-time illegal bookie with mob connections. In 1962 Thorp wrote the preeminent bestseller "Beat the Dealer: A Winning Strategy for the Game of Twenty-One."

To beat the roulette at Las Vegas, he and Claude Shannon, the founder of information theory, invented the first wearable computer in 1961. His success promptly led the casinos to "strongly discourage" him from playing.

In the early sixties, Thorp launched Convertible Hedge Associates, later renamed Princeton Newport Partners, one of the first quantitative hedge funds. The fund had an unrivaled track record following its inception. For 19 years, it had only three down months, with returns exceeding 20 percent over more than three decades. Princeton Newport was wrongly charged with financial misconduct in connection with Drexel Burnham Lambert's junk bond schemes in the 1980s. The fund and his partners were cleared of any wrongdoing, but the financial burden of the investigation led to it being shut down.

Thorp is currently based in Newport Beach in California and serves as president of Edward O. Thorp & Associates. His net worth is close to $1 billion.

He has written some books, his most recent being the much-acclaimed auto-biographical bestseller "A Man for All Markets: From Las Vegas to Wall Street, How I Beat the Dealer and the Market."

His other books include "Beat the Market: A Scientific Stock Market System," "The Mathematics of Gambling," "The Kelly Capital Growth Investment Criterion" and "Elementary probability."

1

The intelligent investor is a realist who sells to optimists and buys from pessimists.

— BENJAMIN GRAHAM

	2	3	1			7	5	8
1	9	4	5	8	6			
		5		6	2	4	1	9
4		9	7			3	6	
8				6				1
				4		8	7	
			1			5	8	7
9			5		7		3	
5					3	1		

336

2

Gentlemen prefer bonds.

— ANDREW MELLON

			5	2			6	1
5			1	3	6	7		4
	3							
		3		5				
	5		6	1	2	4	3	
6		2		4		5	7	9
		5			1			
3		1	7	9				
7						8	1	3

337

3

It is one of the great paradoxes of the stock market that what seems too high usually goes higher and what seems too low usually goes lower.

— WILLIAM O'NEIL

			1		6		2	7
1			7		2	5	4	9
		2		5		6		
	7	3	4	9			5	6
			6	1				
				7	3	8		
	6	9	3		1			
			8			6		5
8	4	7	5	6		2		3

338

4

Be who you are and say what you feel, because those who mind don't matter and those who matter don't mind.

— BERNARD BARUCH

			6	1		9		5
	6		9	2		8	3	
				3	4			7
5						8		
4		7			1	5	6	2
		8			2			
8	1	4		7		3		
6		7	3	5	9	1	4	8
9		5						6

339

5

Don't think there are no crocodiles because the water is calm.

— MALAYAN PROVERB

5	2			6		4		
7							5	
1	8		2		5			
6	1			2	4		9	7
	5			3	9		6	
		3	1		6	2		
3	6			5		7	2	
8				7		1	3	
		9		1	3		8	4

340

6

Bottoms in the investment world don't end with four-year lows; they end with 10- or 15-year lows.

— JIM ROGERS

	9						2	
4		7	1			6	5	9
1					6	4		
3	1		6	5		9	7	4
	5	2		4			3	
	4	9					6	5
9		5			4			6
8	3	4	2					
		1	9	7		4		

341

7

A man in a hot air balloon realized he was lost. The balloonist reduced his altitude and saw a man below.

Balloonist: "Excuse me, but can you help me? I promised a friend I would meet him an hour ago, but I don't know where I am."

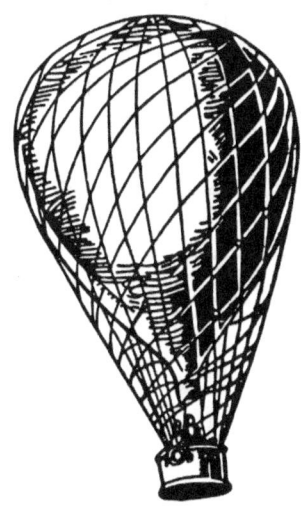

HUBARATO SAIKARO

Man on the ground: "You are in a hot air balloon hovering approximately 30 feet above the ground. You are between 40 and 41 degrees North latitude and between 56 and 57 degrees West longitude."

Balloonist: "You must be a broker."

Man on the ground: "I am, but how did you know?"

Balloonist: "Everything you told me is technically correct, but I have no idea what to make of your information, and the fact is I'm still lost. Frankly, you've not been much help so far."

Man on the ground: "You must be a trader."

Balloonist: "Yes, I am, but how did you know?"

Man on the ground: "You don't know where you are or where you are going. You have risen to your current position due to a large quantity of hot air. You made a promise which you have no idea how to keep, and you expect me to solve your problem. The fact is, you are in the same position you were in before we met, but now, somehow, it's my fault."

— UNKNOWN

9	3	7	2	6	1		4	8
				8		7		
7	9	3		2			5	4
	2	6	4	8		3	7	
4	8				3	6	1	2
					2	8		
6	1	2				3		
5				9	3	2	6	

342

8

When I was young people called me a gambler. As the scale of my operations increased, I became known as a speculator. Now I am called a banker. But I have been doing the same things all the time.

— ERNEST CASSEL

		3						5
			7		5	3	8	4
2			4	3		7	9	6
				6	7	1		
	9	6		2	5	4		8
1		5		4				9
5		2	3			6	7	
			7		6	2	5	
6				1	2	8	4	3

342

9

Amateurs look for challenges; professionals look for easy trades. Losers get high from the action; the pros look for the best odds.

— ALEXANDER ELDER

			5	9	2		6	8	
2	1			6	8		5	9	4
			8	4		9	2		
				4	5	7	2		
9	4					1	3		
			1		6			5	9
6	8			5		4	1	7	
5			4	1				3	
1					3			4	

345

10

You don't have to get in or out of a position all at once. Avoid the temptation of wanting to be completely right.

— JACK SCHWAGER

	7	1					9	
				9	4	1		7
					7			3
		3		2	5		1	
		4	7	1				8
9		7	3		8		2	5
	6	5	4				3	1
	2			8		1	5	4
	1	8	3		4		9	2

346

11

Whenever I see "Economists Predict...," I skip ahead to the next paragraph.

— HARRY MARKOWITZ

4	2	9		7	8		3	
8	5	7	6		3		4	2
	6				4	7		
	3					6		8
		5		6		2	9	
	8	6	3		9			
5		4			6	3	2	
6	7					4	5	9
2		3		4		8		7

347

12

Just about everything is cyclical.

— HOWARD MARKS

4	2	7		8	3			6
3	1		9					7
				7				8
6	4							
7		1	5		8		4	2
8	5			2			3	
	6	4	7					
2						9	6	4
1	8	5		4		2		3

348

13

I don't think you can consistently be a winning trader if you're banking on being right more than 50 percent of the time. You have to figure out how to make money being right only 20 to 30 percent of the time.

— BILL LIPSCHUTZ

349

14

If your system isn't any good, you're still going to lose money, no matter how effective your money management rules are. But if you have an approach that makes money, then money management can make the difference between success and failure.

— MONROE TROUT

15

Far more money has been lost by investors preparing for corrections, or trying to anticipate corrections, than has been lost in corrections themselves.

— PETER LYNCH

	3		8	6		7		
		6	7	4		2		
	7	4			3	6	9	
				7	4		2	5
				2				9
2		3	9	8			7	4
		5		9		1		
				1		5		2
7		1	5		2			

351

16

The two most difficult things at the stock market are to accept a loss and not to realize a small profit.

— ANDRÉ KOSTOLANY

3					8	7		
6			5	4				
	7	5				8		
2				9	4		5	
8	6	9		5	4			
5	4	7				9	8	
1	2	3	8		4			
	8			5	2			
7		4	3	2			9	

352

17

There are too many unpredictable things that can happen within two months. To me, the ideal trade lasts ten days, but I approach every trade as if I'm only going to hold it two or three days.

— LINDA BRADFORD RASCHKE

9	1	3		8	2			4
8	2	7	5				1	3
4	5	6		3	9			
7	8	2						
				9		8		7
3				2		4	5	
		4	3	9			8	2
1		9	8	2	7			
2		8	6			1	3	

353

18

The mistakes we make as investors is when the market's going up, we think it's going to go up forever. When the market goes down, we think it's going to go down forever. Neither of those things actually happen.

— JACK BOGLE

			1	4	2			
3								
4		1			8	3	5	
9	8	7		5	6		2	
7		8			5			
	3	5	2	1	4		7	
1	4		8	7	9		3	
	1	4		8	7	5	6	3
8							1	4
								7

354

19

Trading is very competitive, and you have to be able to handle getting your butt kicked.

— PAUL TUDOR JONES

		9			6	7	2	1
			6		2			9
	5	2	9				7	3
2			7	3	4	5	6	1
4	7			5	6			
		1				3		
3	6	1	2	8	5	7		4
5				4	7	9	3	6
9		7						

355

20

A dollar picked up in the road is more satisfaction to us than the 99 which we had to work for, and the money won at Faro or in the stock market snuggles into our hearts in the same way.

— MARK TWAIN

			3			4	5	
		8	4					
	5	7	9	2				
8					1	6		
	9		6		5	8	4	
6	3		8					
	7		2	6	4	1		
		3	4	1	8	9		7
		4			7			6

356

21

I wait until an investment idea is so good, it hits me over the head like an anvil.

— JOEL GREENBLATT

6				2	3			4
	2				4			
4		5	7					
	3	8	4	7		6		
1		7	6		9	3		5
	6		3	8	5		7	1
	9		5	4		1		2
7	5							8
		6	9	3				

357

22

It can be very expensive to try to convince the markets you are right.

— ED SEYKOTA

			9	4	6	8		7	
		6			5	7	1		
3	5	7	2			6			
9			5	8					
				3	6		5	9	
				2					
1		2		7	4			5	
6	7	4	5	9	3	8			
5	9	3			2		4		

358

23

Place your stops at a point that, if reached, will reasonably indicate that the trade is wrong, not at a point determined primarily by the maximum dollar amount you are willing to lose.

— BRUCE KOVNER

5				8	3			
	9	8				5		2
	7					3	9	
8	6	7		4	5			
	5	1	9	2		8		7
		9	7				5	
				1	2	9	8	
1		3		9	8		4	
		6	5	7			2	3

359

24

Don't fight the Fed.

— WALL STREET SAYING

		1			9		2	7
				2		6	1		3
6	2	7		1		4		8
7		2		3		8		
	5	3	9		4	7	6	
		9					1	
3		5	4					
9	8	4					3	1
2		6	1	5			8	

360

25

A good rule of thumb for many things in life holds that things take longer to happen than you think they will, and then happen faster than you thought they could.

— LAWRENCE SUMMERS

	5			4	9	2		1
4	9			1				
1	2	6	7		8			9
6	1		8				3	
8	7	5	9			1	2	
					1			
	8	7				1		2
9	3			2		5		8
		6	5	8		9		

351

26

The secret of business is to know something that nobody else knows.

— ARISTOTLE ONASSIS

		5	3	1	6	2	8	9
	6							
8	9	2			5	1		
5		7				2		
	1	6		2		4		
					3			
7	5		1	6	3		9	2
			8	9		7	5	
9		8	7		4	6	3	

362

27

In the real world, illiquid assets carry a discount.

— DAVID EINHORN

4	9	2						
		7	5		1	2	4	9
		1	4		2	7	8	3
			7	8				
7	8					6	2	
		3	2		6		7	
9						5		2
3	1			6		5	4	
6				7		8	3	1

363

28

The average man doesn't wish to be told that it is a bull or a bear market. What he desires is to be told specifically which particular stock to buy or sell. He wants to get something for nothing. He does not wish to work. He doesn't even wish to have to think.

— JESSE LIVERMORE

			6	7		2	9	
	7			9	8		5	
-	9	1	5		6		3
				2			1	5
			8		5		6	7
		1	4	6				
		3	9			5	4	
1	9	8	5	4	6	7	3	
6	5				2		8	1

364

29

Work eight hours and sleep eight hours, and make sure that they are not the same eight hours.

— T. BOONE PICKENS

			1		2	4	6	
2	1		7					5
		7			8		2	
			8	3		1	9	
	8			1	9			6
			6	7			8	3
	7		5	8		2	1	9
3					2	6	7	4
1	9	2	4	6	7			8

365

30

Money is the opposite of the weather. Nobody talks about it, but everybody does something about it.

— REBECCA JOHNSON

```
3     |     7 | 2   4
7 5   |     4 | 1
    4 |       |     9
------+-------+------
9   5 |   2   | 8 1 3
      |       | 9 7
1     |   5   | 4 2 6
------+-------+------
8 1 3 |       |
5 9   | 6 4 2 |   8
  4 2 |   1   | 5
```

366

31

I insist on a lot of time being spent, almost every day, to just sit and think.

That is very uncommon in American business. I read and think. So, I do more reading and thinking, and make less impulse decisions than most people in business. I do it because I like this kind of life.

— WARREN BUFFETT

2				4				9
			9	5		7	2	1
	9	5		1				6
3	6			9		1	7	2
			7	2				
7				6		9	5	
	5			7		3	6	
	7		3		6		9	
			8	9	2			7

344

ABOUT THE AUTHOR

Hubarato Saiko has an extensive experience in the stock market, having started trading in 1987. What began as a hobby quickly turned into a lucrative secondary source of income. As Hubarato's trading skills and profits grew, he soon found himself earning more from trading than from his corporate salary. This pivotal moment prompted him to make a life-changing decision to become a full-time trader.

Since then, Hubarato has dedicated himself entirely to the world of trading and has never looked back. He has honed his trading strategies and developed a deep understanding of the market dynamics. With his unwavering passion and determination, Hubarato has achieved remarkable success in the financial industry.

Currently residing in southern Spain, Hubarato operates his own family office, overseeing his trading activities and managing his investment portfolio. His expertise and disciplined approach to trading have garnered him a reputation as a skilled and knowledgeable trader. Hubarato continues to thrive in the challenging world of finance, always seeking new opportunities and staying ahead of the ever-changing market trends.

BOOKS BY HUBARATO SAIKARO

SOLUTIONS

A PDF containing the puzzles and their solutions can be downloaded from:
https://drive.proton.me/urls/EW14NN951W#aPoBCmuEIUII

www.ingramcontent.com/pod-product-compliance
Lightning Source LLC
Chambersburg PA
CBHW071443220526
45472CB00003B/650